INTEGRATION OF SPECIAL HOSPITAL PATIENTS INTO THE COMMUNITY

Integration of Special Hospital Patients into the Community

MARGARET NORRIS
Research Fellow
Department of Sociology,
University of Surrey

Gower

Published by
Gower Publishing Company Limited,
Gower House, Croft Road, Aldershot, Hants GU11 3HR,
England

and

Gower Publishing Company,
Old Post Road, Brookfield,
Vermont 05036, U.S.A.

British Library Cataloguing in Publication Data

Norris, Margaret
    Integration of special hospital patients
    into the community.
    1. Psychiatric hospital patients——
    Rehabilitation——Great Britain
    2. Insane, Criminal and dangerous——
    Rehabilitation——Great Britain
    I. Title
    362.2'1   RC439.5

    ISBN 0-566-00728-2

Printed and bound in Great Britain by
Antony Rowe Limited, Chippenham, Wilts.

Contents

Tables

Please note: Throughout this book row percentages, across the page, are shown in brackets (%) but column percentages, down the page, are shown in square brackets [%]. Because of rounding, percentages occasionally do not total exactly 100.

Acknowledgements

The research on which this book is based was funded by the Department of Health and Social Security. Broadmoor and other Special Hospital staff, Home Office personnel, doctors, probation officers, social workers and especially patients discharged from the Special Hospital who collaborated in the project are thanked for their assistance. The project benefited from help from many other people, too numerous to mention by name, to whom I am indebted. In particular it would not have begun without the encouragement of Tony Black, Consultant Psychologist at Broadmoor, and would not have been completed without the assistance of Jane Fielding, Brian Haddon, Gloria Lopez and Fay Prosser, whose contributions were invaluable.

1 Introduction: patients leaving the hospital

Introduction

This book describes the careers of men who left a Special Hospital between 1974 and 1981. Many aspects of patients' histories were examined to see which events or characteristics were associated with successful resettlement in the community.

There are four Special Hospitals in England. Their patients are often described as 'abnormal offenders', although about a fifth of them have not been referred as the result of conviction for any imprisonable offence. All are compulsorily detained, usually as the result of a Hospital Order made during a court appearance but some come directly from prison or from an ordinary psychiatric hospital (referred to hereafter as 'NHS hospital'). To qualify for admission patients must be thought sufficiently dangerous to themselves or others to require conditions of special security; and likely to benefit from hospital treatment because they suffer from mental illness or a personality disorder or psychopathy.

Apart from one study by Black (1982) of records of men who were conditionally or absolutely discharged from Broadmoor during 1960–1965, there has been little research into the postdischarge careers of Special Hospital patients. Walker and McCabe (1973) included 24 such patients in a two year follow up study, but Freeman and Simmons (1963) concluded from their study of American psychiatric patients that this was too short a period to provide useful information.

1

Acres (1975) studied 92 Special Hospital patients who had been in the community for three years but, perhaps because of pressures of time since the report was prepared for the Butler Committee (HMSO, 1975), his sample was unrepresentative. Amongst some other American studies (e.g. Thornberry and Jacoby, 1979; and Zitrin et al., 1976) dealing with discharged psychiatric hospital patients in the community, only Thornberry and Jacoby used a follow up period as long as four years. Their patients had characteristics similar to men discharged from Special Hospitals but only 44 per cent of 586 patients were traced and only 17 per cent interviewed in the community. These American patients also lacked the kind of official aftercare which was mandatory for the majority of discharged Special Hospital patients in the United Kingdom.

Characteristics of patients were believed to have changed since Black's patients left the Special Hospital and there was no information at all about the subsequent progress of the majority of patients, those who entered the community after first being transferred to an ordinary hospital or another custodial institution. More comprehensive and up to date analysis of the British patients was needed if discharge, rehabilitation and aftercare were to be based on accurate information.

A four year study of all those 588 men who left Broadmoor for the first time between 1974 and 1981 was therefore designed to provide information about factors associated with the successful reintegration into the community of male Special Hospital patients of normal intelligence. The findings reported here cannot be generalised to women or mentally impaired men who have other very different characteristics from the men studied.

What constitutes successful reintegration?

The concept of 'successful reintegration into the community' is used since it describes the situation patients hoped to reach, one in which they were indistinguishable from other members of the public. It also avoids the confusion caused by differing usages of 'rehabilitation' amongst those responsible for aftercare. 'Resocialisation', an alternative used by some forensic psychiatrists, suggests rather more active intervention than was anticipated by patients or their helpers in this study.

Special Hospital patients were admitted because their behaviour was regarded as dangerously unmanageable or intolerable in other milieux. It is possible that treatment in a Special Hospital might completely reform the lifestyle of a patient, a view which seems to be implicit in measures of reintegration relying on recidivism or readmission to hospital as indicators of failure. Most Special Hospital doctors considered that their function was limited to treating the illness diagnosed at the time of the patient's admission; they would recommend discharge or transfer when symptoms were cured or controlled to a degree which would prevent the recurrence of previously unacceptable behaviour and the patient was rehabilitated in the clinical sense.

More comprehensive preparation for reentry to the community was not part of Special Hospital policy for men during the period studied. Consultants there, in keeping with recommendations in the Butler Committee's Report on Abnormal Offenders (HMSO, 1975), expected any rehabilitation or resocialisation which a patient might require after a long stay in an enclosed institution to take place after the patient left the Special Hospital (see also the Hospital Advisory Service report, cited by Gostin, 1977).

Bowden (1981) argued that preadmission histories are the most reliable indicators of post discharge deviant behaviour, which suggests that preadmission lifestyles do remain relatively unaffected by treatment. After discharge well adjusted patients may comfortably resettle in a familiar environment although this may be deviant or disorganised by the standards of doctors and social supervisors (a blanket term used in this book to include probation officers, social workers, community nurses, hostel wardens, and others involved in aftercare). The Special Hospital would nevertheless have fulfilled the expectations which society has about treatment if discharged or transferred patients were able to avoid the kind of deviant behaviour which precipitated their admission. Reintegration into the community would therefore be partially achieved if patients continued to avoid such behaviour.

However, reintegration into community life also requires a level of independent functioning and this may be difficult for patients discharged from a totally enclosed environment to achieve. Special Hospital consultants in fact did not generally anticipate more than 'danger free resettlement' for those discharged directly into the community and 'stability in an institution' for those transferred to NHS hospitals. Others responsible for patients after they left the Special Hospital seemed to have higher expectations but anticipated that these would be achieved by slow stages. Social and psychiatric supervision was expected to continue until a patient demonstrated an ability to live independently as well as to avoid the behaviour which precipitated admission. The way in which progress towards this kind of reintegration was identified for research purposes is described in the next chapter.

Social factors

Freeman and Simmons (1963) and Zitrin and colleagues (1976) concluded that social factors, not objective differences in social adjustment, led to recall and conviction. Bowden's (1981) review stressed the importance of preadmission histories for postdischarge careers. Patients' individual characteristics were also very likely to affect their progress. In addition, if problems resulted from institutionalisation, lengths of stay in the Special and other hospitals might be of paramount importance. Other factors thought to affect postdischarge progress were mentioned by respondents to interviews or discussed in case histories. All these factors needed to be investigated.

The patients studied and how they left Broadmoor

The study began in January 1979 and a review of the figures for men leaving in the previous decade suggested that a sufficient sample would be available if data collection included all those leaving between January 1974 and January 1981. However, it was known that some patients were recalled and discharged later, sometimes on more than one occasion, although since a new hospital number is allocated at each admission this is not readily apparent from official records. A fifth of all 'separations' were found to be second or subsequent departures, this 'revolving door' aspect of Broadmoor having doubled since the early 1960s. Only patients whose first departure was within the research period were included so that complete careers were investigated and so that some confusions inherent in earlier studies and possibly also in official statistics could be avoided. (For example, the use of hospital numbers leads to duplication of data for the same individual and to distortions of mean age at departure and of length of stay as these refer to the latest period in hospital). The careers of some patients who left for the first time during the research period did, of course, include recalls and subsequent discharges.

The 588 men who left for the first time were 'separated' in the manner and at the times shown in Table 1.1 opposite. The research period was extended to May 1981 because the number of departures was smaller than anticipated. The fall partially reflects a constant trend since the beginning of the 1960s, similar to that in all psychiatric hospitals, when changes in treatment and policy led to the discharge of many patients who were well able to cope in the community. When the initial backlog was cleared the annual rates of discharge fell but there has been a more marked decrease in recent years. This is more apparent when the transfers to other Special Hospitals, mainly to reduce overcrowding, are disregarded. The annual mean for all other first time separations in the years 1974–1978 is 72; the annual mean for similar separations during 1979–1981 is 42.

The fall is not due to a decrease in the base rate, that is to the decreasing number of patients in Broadmoor, since in that case separations would have fallen more sharply in 1976. Dell's (1980) findings on the length of time patients wait for discharge refute any suggestion that fewer patients were ready for discharge. A decline in intake by NHS hospitals is not solely responsible since the numbers being discharged directly into the community also diminished over the period. Changes amongst the small number of consultants responsible for recommending discharge might affect Special Hospital policy; but no staff changes of this kind occurred until after the research period ended.

Table 1.1
Mode of separation from Broadmoor (N 588)

Year	CD[*]	AD[*]	NHS	Other SH	HMP	Dead	Dep/ Rep	Yearly totals
1974	17	3	44	32	2	8	4	110
1975	7	7	47	34	2	8	3	108
1976	12	7	35	8	5	5	3	75
1977	18	3	37	9	2	5	5	79
1978	16	4	39	28	4	5	3	99
1979	12	4	22	1	1	4	2	46
1980	9	1	18	6	2	–	2	38
1981 (part)	3	1	17	11	–	1	–	33
Total	94	30	259	129	18	36	22	588
Per cent	(16)	(5)	(44)	(22)	(3)	(6)	(4)	(100)

[*]Discharged directly into the community: see text for explanations of column headings.

The decrease might be explained by a change in policy of a new government, especially if this was influenced by hardening public attitudes (see Norris, 1978). In addition, the economic recession probably resulted in a reduction of possible placements. Some hostels closed for lack of funds during the research period; and short staffed hospitals may be reluctant to accept Special Hospital patients, not necessarily because they are troublesome, but because their stays are expected to be prolonged and strain resources.

The manner in which patients were 'separated' is shown in Table 1.1. Details of those who were 'separated' by death were retained for comparison with the ages, lengths of stay and causes of death of the remainder of the patients studied. A few of the patients who were repatriated (Rep) or deported (Dep) returned to this country and are included in the study. A few were returned to prison (HMP) after treatment. Some were transferred to other Special Hospitals (Other SH), mainly for administrative reasons.

44 per cent were transferred to NHS hospitals (NHS) in the manner recommended by the Butler (HMSO, 1975) and Aarvold (HMSO, 1973)

5

Committees. If only patients discharged into the community or transferred to NHS hospitals are considered, 31 per cent took a path which was regarded as one which should be 'exceptional' by the Aarvold Committee. These patients were discharged either 'conditionally' (CD) or 'absolutely' (AD) directly into the community. Conditionally discharged patients were still subject to conditions of a Restriction Order made by the Court at the same time as the Hospital Order for their admission. Conditions usually included a requirement that a patient should accept medical and social supervision after discharge and should reside at a known address. Such supervision included powers to recommend recall to a Special Hospital without further recourse to the courts, a procedure which has attracted censure from the European Commission for Human Rights. The majority of absolutely discharged patients had never been subject to a Court Order, although in some cases a Restriction Order had expired during their stay in the hospital. In recent years most Restriction Orders have been made 'without limit of time' and can only be discharged by a warrant from the Home Secretary, a practice more frequently adopted for patients in the community during the last two or three years of the research period. Absolutely discharged patients left the Special Hospital in much the same way as any recovered patient would leave any ordinary hospital.

Patients transferred to NHS hospitals, but not those returned to prison, might remain subject to a Restriction Order which would affect the way in which they eventually returned to the community. A few patients having intermittent or very brief leave were omitted from this study, but patients on leave for more than three months preceding discharge (during which time they was supervised and subject to recall) were included.

Conditions which make supervision mandatory may appear desirable, facilitating, for example, the discharge of patients whose illness is thought to be controlled only by medication. If no supervision were available it might be thought against the public interest for some patients ever to be discharged. On the other hand, conditions may be perceived to be stigmatic and disruptive of the relationship between patient and supervisor. Comparisons between the careers of the restricted and unrestricted patients were planned to investigate possible differences.

Summary

The reasons for undertaking the study have been explained. Some information has been given about the numbers of patients studied and the manner in which they were 'separated' from the hospital. Two particularly interesting facts emerged. One was the small number of patients leaving Broadmoor for the first time. Hospitals and receiving agencies seem unlikely to be overwhelmed by this increase

6

in their total annual workload. The second was the unexpectedly high proportion of patients who had no opportunity for rehabilitation in an NHS hospital.

2 Patients found and assessed in the community

Data collection

Information about patients was obtained from interviews and repertory grids (described later) completed by patients; from interviews with patients' supervisors (psychiatrists and 'social supervisors'); from questionnaires completed by the supervisors whose only responsibility was for inpatients; and from case histories and other documentary sources. 'Hard data', including information about patients' characteristics, pre-admission history, stays in hospital and postdischarge history were used in quantitative analysis (details of schedules and categorisation are available for examination in Norris, 1983b). Qualitative analysis of 'soft data' (see Norris, 1981) was used to identify and examine 'frequently recurring topics' in source material. Issues of interest and concern to respondents were pinpointed by this method which also facilitated categorisation and interpretation of quantitative material.

A rather tortuous approach to patients was arranged in order to resolve some ethical problems. (All those followed up are referred to as 'patients' for convenience; all were expatients of Broadmoor; some were still patients in other Special Hospitals or NHS hospitals; some were expatients of both Special and NHS hospitals; some were outpatients; about three-quarters of these men could accurately be described as patients at the date of interview). Documentary sources were examined first, to assist in tracing patients and identifying last known supervisors. Any doctor treating a patient was asked to confirm that there was no clinical objection to a research session. Of 170 doctors identified as responsible for a patient who had been living or working in the community, only three did not cooperate. In one case this debarred any further approach to the patient. 82 per cent of doctors asked to complete a questionnaire about patients still in hospital cooperated.

The patient was then asked to cooperate by a third party already familiar with his background. The doctor responsible was not asked to make this request in case there was any suggestion of duress. The intermediary was usually a current or recent social supervisor who was also interviewed after agreement had been obtained from any agency for which he or she worked. 224 social supervisors were interviewed about 294 patients who were or had been clients. Four refused, and this debarred access to their clients.

147 patients cooperated in a research session and 145 completed a form of repertory grid designed to investigate patient integration into the community and relationships with family, peers and official helpers. The use of the grid and the preliminary collection of 'hard data' from other sources were planned to avoid approaches which might distress or disturb patients. In the event, many patients wanted to discuss their experiences at much greater length even though this was occasionally distressing. Log notes were kept of 'soft data' volunteered by patients and other respondents during interviews.

Patient response rate was high although those very recently discharged were more likely to refuse. When this was the first decision to be uncooperative which a patient had made since discharge, supervisors were inclined to think this a healthy sign of increasing independence which should not be discouraged. Altogether 32 refused to be interviewed but almost all gave the supervisor permission to discuss their cases with the research worker. Nine other patients were either too heavily medicated, too elderly or spoke too little English for interviews to be fruitful. Another was omitted for ethical reasons and one was taken into custody before interview arrangements had been completed. There was no suitable intermediary for 26 patients. Either a doctor or social supervisor thought it unwise for an approach to be made to 16 patients.

In all 83 per cent of patients capable of responding and who could be approached through an intermediary were interviewed. Very full information was available for 92 per cent of those in the community and some information was available for 11 of the remaining 15 patients in the community who were unrestricted and had never come to official attention. No information was recorded if it was thought that a patient fully informed of the project would have objected to its use or if such information was thought likely to harm a patient or any other respondent; stringent safeguards were adopted to preserve confidentiality. Data were coded so that only the author can identify individuals by means of a key which will be destroyed when some analysis still in hand is completed.

Very few discrepancies between sources were found on matters of 'fact', dates, sequences of events, and biographical details recorded as 'hard data'. There were, of course, many differences in perceptions of situations and events.

Methods of identifying reintegration

Practitioners reading this book will be more interested in the results of the study than in the methods used. The description of the way in which information was collected is given to enable readers to judge for themselves the reliability of the findings. To avoid overloading the text with technical details, more detailed descriptions of the two main approaches to the identification of reintegration described below are provided in an appendix (Appendix One).

Briefly, measures intended to cover the spectrum of possible interpretations of reintegration into the community were devised. For one set of measures the more conventional, but negative, indicators of relapse and recidivism were used. These included informal and formal readmissions and recalls to hospital, suicide and attempted suicide, offences and imprisonment. Patients were then grouped according to the number of incidents in which they had been involved, or the gravity (according to a point system) of incidents in which they had been involved.

Individuals involved in incidents

Being in a custodial institution or in hospital did not prevent a patient from reoffending. About a third of all offences including four of the most serious postdischarge offences committed by patients (two homicidal and two sexual offences) occurred in these environments. However, the majority of offences were petty thefts or money making activities - one patient set up a car repair service in the hospital grounds and another sold hospital crockery and cutlery. Financial problems of patients are discussed later. The number of individuals involved was relatively small: of a total of 112 patients who appeared in court only 22 were not living or working in the community. 40 NHS hospital doctors stated unequivocally that patients from Broadmoor were no more troublesome than any other patients. Of 49 patients reported to be troublesome, four were a danger to themselves rather than to others; ten were a real management problem but four of them were recalled; and the majority of problems which doctors reported as troublesome were related to patients' institutionalisation or to bureaucratic requirements concerning discharge.

The main focus of the study was on 330 'active' patients who had lived or worked in the community. For these patients the numbers and percentages involved (or not) in the various categories of incidents described above are shown in Table 2.1.

Table 2.1
Active patients involved in 'incidents' (N 330)

Number of occasions	None	One	Two or more
Psychiatric incidents	207 (63%)	76 (23%)	47 (14%)
Criminal incidents	240 (73%)	53 (16%)	37 (11%)
Total incidents	161 (49%)	69 (21%)	100 (30%)

Gravity of incident	Nil	Low	High
Psychiatric weighted incidents	207 (63%)	50 (15%)	73 (22%)
Criminal weighted incidents	240 (73%)	38 (12%)	52 (16%)
Total weighted incidents	161 (49%)	71 (21%)	98 (30%)

The overlap between criminal and psychiatric incidents is relatively small, only 44 individuals being involved in both. Fourteen of the individuals involved in psychiatric incidents committed suicide. These, added to a number of attempted suicides, inflate the percentage of grave psychiatric and total incidents although these patients were not a danger to others. A number of offences of assault, also always classified as 'grave', were technical offences and not dangerous incidents. More accurate classification of offences as dangerous or not would require a separate and detailed study. The aim of this project was to cover as many facets of post discharge careers as possible and fine distinctions between types of incidents were not attempted.

Individual repertory grid scores

In addition to indicators of relapse and recidivism, a more positive scale was generated by analysing those sections of the repertory grid which investigated patient attitudes towards rulebreaking, dependency and self esteem.

The scale included seven separate aspects of reintegration:
(1) Patient's self esteem was higher (or lower) than at discharge.
(2) Patient aspired not to break rules (or the reverse).
(3) Patient saw himself as not breaking rules (or the reverse).
(4) Patient saw himself as breaking less (or more) rules than when he left Broadmoor.
(5) Patient aspired to be independent (or the reverse).
(6) Patient saw himself as independent (or the reverse).
(7) Patient saw himself as more (or less) independent than when he left Broadmoor.

A point was given for achieving the desired goal on each aspect. High scores on that scale were found to be associated with fewer of the more familiar negative indicators, in keeping with theoretical and empirical studies which supported the view that such attitudes are associated with nondeviant behaviour, see for example Reckless 1957, 1960, 1961; Reckless and Dinitz, 1967; Schwarz and Tangri, 1965; Kaplan, 1976. A very similar scale, excluding aspects (4) and (7), had been found to coincide with clinical impressions in an earlier study (Norris, 1983a).

Table 2.2
Grid scores for 145 patients

Score	7	6	5	4	3	2	1	0
Number	21	23	31	29	22	13	6	0

Per cent (15) (16) (21) (20) (15) (9) (4) (0)

There were no nil scores and few low scores, predictable if low scorers were recalled, or remained in NHS hospitals, or if patients (or their supervisors on their behalf) refused to cooperate because patient grasp on community life was precarious. For most subsequent analysis it was convenient to divide patients into two groups of about equal numbers, low scorers with four or less points, high scorers with five or more points.

Grid scores were significantly associated with involvement in incidents indicating relapse and recidivism. A strong association had not been anticipated, since the grid was measuring positive aspects of integration as well as the negative aspects reflected by incidents, but an expectation that patients with low scores would be more likely to be involved in incidents was confirmed, see Table 2.3.

Table 2.3
Grid scores by involvement in incidents (N 145)

	Incidents	No incidents	Total
Patients scoring 0-2	14 (74%)	5 (26%)	19 (100%)
Patients scoring 3-4	22 (45%)	29 (54%)	51 (100%)
Patients scoring 5-7	24 (32%)	51 (68%)	75 (100%)
Total	60 (41%)	85 (59%)	145 (100%)

x^2=10.96, df 2, p<.05, Cramer's V .24

There was less overall agreement between grid measures and supervisors' assessments than in earlier studies using similar grid methodology. Reasons for this became apparent later when lack of contact and lack of continuity of contact between supervisors and

patients were disclosed. Despite this there was a 65 per cent
agreement between grid scores and clinical impressions of
schizophrenics. The terms 'psychopaths' and 'schizophrenics' are
reluctantly employed as brief and readily comprehensible descriptions
of two major categories of patients discussed more fully later. It
would be accurate and more in keeping with the dignity of the
patients to refer on each occasion to 'expatients with a diagnosis
which resulted in an allocation to the group labelled psychopathic
(or schizophrenic)'.

Doctors thought that 72 per cent of all their patients were 'doing
well' and 28 per cent 'doing less well'. If patients who scored 4 or
more are included in the 'better integrated' group this results in a
similar 72 per cent and 25 per cent dichotomy instead of the roughly
equal division described above. The arbitrary allocation to
relatively better and less well integrated groups for comparative
purposes does not imply some absolute standard of integration; all
analysis was in fact run using both dichotomies with little effect on
trends in reported results, see for example Table 2.4. However, the
division into equal halves gives a slightly stronger association
between scores and incidents and the more unequal division often
resulted in rather small numbers in the 'less well integrated' group.
The latter dichotomy is therefore only reported when doctors'
impressions are being considered.

Table 2.4
Comparison of two dichotomies of grid scores

	Dichotomy 1 (accords better with doctors' assessments)		Dichotomy 2 (divides sample into roughly equal halves)	
	1-3	4-7	1-4	5-7
Patients involved in:				
No incidents	17 [41%]	68 [65%]	34 [49%]	51 [68%]
Any incidents	24 [59%]	36 [35%]	36 [51%]	24 [32%]
Total	41 [100%]	104 [100%]	70 [100%]	75 [100%]

$$X^2=6.94, \; p<.05, \; phi \; .22 \; : \; X^2=10.16, \; p<.005, \; phi \; .26$$

Doctors were significantly (p<.025) more likely to assess
schizophrenics as 'doing less well' than psychopaths, probably
because they met the former more frequently; this finding is
discussed in more detail later. Moreover, using that dichotomy of
scores which coincides with doctors' perceptions of the proportion
'doing well', psychopaths amongst grid completers were in fact
significantly (p<.005) more likely to be in the 'better integrated'
group than schizophrenics, though not as often as doctors'
assessments suggested.

Social supervisors so rarely thought any patient who remained in the community was not 'doing well' that it was not worth pursuing a similar analysis. However, the fact that social supervisors experienced difficulty in assessing relative degrees of reintegration was thought likely to create difficulties in supervision.

There was a marked association between involvement in incidents and aspirations to break rules; and a significant though not very strong association ($p<.05$; phi .17) between involvement in incidents and self percept as rulebreaking. Although this suggests that these aspects of integration alone are predictive the strength of the associations between aspects and involvement in incidents was weaker than the association between such involvement and total grid scores already shown in Table 2.3. Eight of nine incidents which occurred after grids had been completed involved low scorers (half of whom had scored 1-2). All nine had been assessed by supervisors as 'doing well'. Further follow up is now planned to test the ability of the grids to predict incidents within a specified period.

It was concluded that the grid score accurately reflected the relative degree of integration of patients in the community, although if respondents had not been convinced that their research sessions were confidential they might not have cooperated. Because involvement in incidents of the kind recorded was associated with the grid measure of poorer integration, it was thought reasonable to use such incidents as indicators of poorer integration for patients for whom no grid was available, although no conclusions could then be drawn about the relative degree of positive aspects of integration amongst those not involved in incidents.

Patient status in the community

Most patients were followed up for four years, 31 per cent for more than five years and some for as long as seven or eight years. 71 per cent of interview dates were within three to six years after separation. Table 2.5 opposite shows the status of all patients at the date of interview or at the latest date at which information was available. 'Interview date' was occasionally notional when only documentary evidence was available, but usually refers to the date when the patient or, if not the patient, either his doctor or social supervisor was interviewed. 'Technical inpatients' had not been formally discharged but lived in hospital-owned property in the community or were on extended leave pending permission from the Home Secretary for their formal discharge.

Just sufficient data was analysed for that 28 per cent shown in Table 2.5 as never in the community in the United Kingdom to establish that they had no characteristics which distinguished them in any way which might need to be considered in further analysis. In

Table 2.5
Status of 588 patients at date of interview and of latest information
(Percentages have been rounded)

Status	Number (%) at interview	Number at latest info.
Never in community in U.K. (N 165: 28 per cent)		
Died in Broadmoor	36 [6]	36
In country of origin	19 [3]	19
Died in country of origin	1 [-]	1
Remained in new SH after transfer	94 [16]	92
Died in new SH after transfer	4 [1]	4
Still in HMP	14 [2]	13
NHS patients and others in community (Core sample, N 423):		
Inactive core sample (N 93: 16 per cent)		
Still in NHS after transfer	77 [13]	71
Died in NHS after transfer	18 [3]	22
Active core sample (N 330: 56 per cent)		
In custody: HMP (sentenced)	14 [2]	15
SH (recalled)	28 [5]	35
In hospital:		
Informal readmission	15 [3]	15
Formal readmission	7 [1]	9
In community, restricted:		
Technical inpatient	10 [2]	9
Formally supervised	123 [21]	108
Ditto, social sup. only	16 [3]	17
Died whilst conditionally disch.	11 [2]	11
Day patient	18 [3]	18
Absconded, vol.repat.	4 [1]	4
On leave	1 [-]	1
In community, unrestricted:		
Absolutely disch./all sup. lapsed	43 [9]	53
Voluntary medical sup.	15 [2]	14
Voluntary social sup.	8 [1]	8
Died whilst absolutely discharged	1 [-]	1
Day patient	5 [1]	6
Voluntary repat.	6 [1]	6
TOTAL	588 [101]	588

addition, although the 129 patients transferred to other Special Hospitals had a mean length of stay in Broadmoor shorter than that of other patients, those who subsequently entered the community had a total length of stay in Special Hospitals which was similar to the length of stay of those who entered the community directly from Broadmoor. There was therefore no need to distinguish between the two groups on this account and since their postdischarge careers did not differ significantly it seems probable that reported findings apply to all men of average or above average intelligence leaving any Special Hospital.

It was noteworthy that although a similar number of deaths occured amongst expatients as amongst Broadmoor inmates during the period researched there was a difference in the manner of death. Only six (17 per cent) of the 36 deaths in Broadmoor (Table 1.1) were recorded as from unnatural causes. The population of inmates amongst which these 36 deaths occurred was certainly no smaller than that studied after separation and the total duration of time in which deaths could occur was longer than the total lengths of time during which all discharged patients were followed up. Of 39 expatients who died within the period researched, 18 (of whom only three were under fifty) died from natural causes but 21 (54 per cent, of whom only five were over fifty) from unnatural causes, mostly suicide or in circumstances which suggested suicide, although one was the victim of a murder. There was apparently a much higher rate of suicide amongst discharged patients than amongst patients who remained in Broadmoor.

Subsequent analysis was confined to the remaining 423 patients, the 'core' sample in Table 2.5. The 'inactive' of these (16 per cent of the whole 588) remained or died in the hospital to which they had been transferred, though usually free to come and go whilst inpatients. The remaining 330 'active' patients (56 per cent of the whole 588) lived or worked in the community at some time.

Three-quarters of patients transferred to NHS hospitals had been in the community at some time. Two-thirds were still in the community at the date of interview. So were a quarter of those who had first been transferred to another Special Hospital. Of those who did leave NHS hospitals, 11 per cent did so within three months and 80 per cent within two years.

The number returning to the community was larger and the rate of return faster than had been anticipated by Special Hospital doctors. The number needing rehabilitation was therefore greater than had been anticipated and the length of time spent in NHS hospitals even by those transferred there for rehabilitation was brief by Special Hospital standards. Nearly 40 per cent of the patients studied had been in the Special Hospital for over six years and seven per cent had been there more than 15 years.

Summary

The methods used to obtain information about patients have been described. It has been argued that the grid measure accurately reflects the relative levels of patient reintegration into the community and it may be predictive of incidents of relapse and recidivism. Because low scorers were more likely to be involved in incidents of the kind recorded as indicators of relapse and recidivism, similar incidents could be used to indicate poor integration for patients for whom no grid was available.

In addition to those patients discharged directly into the community, and therefore with no possibility of rehabilitation in an NHS hospital, another large group who had been transferred to NHS hospitals were found to be leaving them after a relatively short time for rehabilitation. A vulnerability to suicide amongst expatients was also noted. A review of some of the more general aspects of patients' careers after leaving Broadmoor follows in the next chapter.

3 Patients' histories, stays in hospital and postdischarge careers

Patient characteristics and preadmission histories

What sort of men left Broadmoor? What had been their previous experience? What were their admission offences, what sort of illnesses did they have?

General characteristics

The majority (61 per cent) of patients were single when admitted. About a fifth were married when admitted but half of these men were divorced by the time of discharge. Another five per cent were widowed, the majority as a result of their admission offence, and fourteen per cent were already divorced or separated when admitted.

Most (83 per cent) were unskilled. Eight per cent had achieved either 'O' or 'A' grades before leaving school but only six per cent had any further education. Although with rare exceptions those who were professionally qualified (three per cent) and the skilled (ten per cent) were in employment at the time of their offence, 34 per cent of all patients were unemployed at that time and another 19 per cent were not working because they were ill or in hospital. Nearly half of all patients had had many or lengthy periods of unemployment, some because of psychiatric illness and some because of the physical disabilities from which 13 per cent suffered on admission. More than half of these physical disabilities were severe and included deafness, near blindness, loss of a limb and chronic disabling illnesses.

A quarter of the men had a history of alcohol abuse and about a third came from disorganised family backgrounds. Family backgrounds were regarded as 'disorganised' only if this had attracted attention and adverse comment from welfare or other agencies, otherwise as 'organised', regardless of their complexity or unconventionality. Nearly a third of all patients came from families where members had a history of admissions to psychiatric hospitals and 11 per cent from families where members had a criminal history but these families were not necessarily 'disorganised'. Examples of 'disorganisation' which had attracted adverse comment included father's incestuous relations with siblings; elder sister mothering a multiply handicapped 'problem' family; parents in prison for child or wife battering; and some parents involved in prostitution, abuse of drugs or alcohol.

Nearly half of all patients were aged less than 30 when admitted. Excluding those patients who were living in hospital and prison for lengthy periods before admission, a third of the remaining 387 patients were living with their parents before admission, a quarter with their wives. 14 per cent of patients lost a close relative (usually a parent) by death during their stay in hospital, two per cent lost both parents by death.

Psychiatric characteristics

There were two main categories of mental illness amongst patients. 59 per cent of all patients were schizophrenic and 27 per cent psychopathic (or personality disordered). Small groups of patients with a variety of mental disorders such as the affective disorders and organic brain damage were at first recorded separately but finally combined to make 14 per cent of 'other mental illnesses' for the purposes of analysis, see for example Table 3.2.

The way in which diagnostic categories are defined affects comparisons with other studies and the categorisation of Special Hospital patients presents more problems than those discussed in the general literature on mental illness. For example, one doctor wrote that he was 'aware of the administrative and functional expediency sometimes relevant in recommending disposal or placement' and that his colleagues could expect to find his diagnosis 'flexible'. For research purposes, patients were categorised as psychopathic when this term or 'personality disordered' was recorded in admission documents. Patients were categorised as schizophrenic when their admission diagnoses used this term, or when their diagnoses referred to psychosis including delusions. When conflicting diagnoses were recorded, categorisation as schizophrenic was made if the patient's symptoms included delusions for which major tranquillisers were prescribed. This is a wider categorisation than some clinicians might approve, since it includes, for example, patients who were reported to have had a brief psychotic episode. However, this system seemed to be justified when analysis using these definitions was compared to some earlier stages of analysis which included only schizophrenics so defined in admission diagnosis. Percentages and significant findings were hardly affected although the numbers involved were increased substantially. Moreover, using this procedure, which resulted in the percentages given above, discharge diagnoses only differed from admission diagnoses by two per cent after allowance had been made for the 'symptom free'.

Criminal characteristics

The two largest categories of admission offences (or offences prior to admission where patients had arrived from prison or another hospital) were assaults (31 per cent) and homicides (27 per cent and there were in addition nine per cent attempted homicides). 16 per cent were for acquisitive or other kinds of offence, mostly not serious. Eight per cent of offences were sexual (including two cases of exhibitionism) and nine per cent were arson, see Table 3.3.

For purposes of analysis an admission offence of 'assault' was attributed to a patient admitted from an NHS hospital because of an attack upon another patient or a member of staff, even when no charge had been made. 'Other' offences also include the noncriminal one of being a management problem in an NHS hospital, other than being assaultive, and may include damage to property and other offences where no charge was brought. In all, four per cent of the total number of offenders in the analyses which follow had not been charged with the offence attributed to them. Their inclusion was thought justifiable since their histories were likely to influence their future careers; and it is apparently customary in research concerning Special Hospital patients to categorise as an offence an alleged crime where no trial was held because the patient was found unfit to plead.

A fifth of the patients had been admitted to custodial institutions before adulthood and about a third had had numerous court appearances as adults, mostly for acquisitive or 'other' offences, usually relatively trivial.

Combined psychiatric and criminal histories

About two-thirds of all patients had a preadmission criminal history and the same proportion had a psychiatric record but only 11 per cent had neither criminal nor psychiatric record and nearly 40 per cent had both. Patients from disorganised families were more likely to have preadmission histories of deviant behaviour, see Table 3.1 opposite.

Table 3.1
Preadmission history by family organisation where known (N477)

History	Organised	Disorganised	Total (% of 477)
Court appearances + hosp. admits.	122 (65%)	66 (35%)	188 [39%]
Court appearances only	81 (63%)	40 (37%)	121 [25%]
Hospital admissions only	91 (78%)	26 (22%)	117 [25%]
None known	45 (88%)	6 (12%)	51 [11%]
Total	339 (71%)	138 (29%)	477 (100%)

$$X^2=16.94, \text{ df } 3, \text{ p}<.001; \text{ Cramer's V } .19$$

So, on arrival in Broadmoor the majority of patients were single, relatively young, and had some previous history of deviant behaviour, though for about a third the crime which led to admission was a first offence. Many had disorganised homes and histories of unemployment; a sizeable proportion had drinking problems or physical disabilities.

Factors associated with lengths of stay in hospital and modes of discharge

Long stays in the Special Hospital were common and lengths of stay were strongly associated with admission offence (see Table 3.3 overleaf) but not with diagnosis (see Table 3.2 below where X^2 is not significant).

Table 3.2
Diagnosis by length of stay in Special Hospital (N 588)

Length of stay	Psych.	Schiz.	Other	Total
> 3 years	43 [29%]	104 [30%]	24 [29%]	171 [29%]
3 > 6 years	52 [33%]	100 [29%]	27 [30%]	179 [30%]
< 6 years	62 [39%]	143 [41%]	33 [40%]	238 [40%]
Total	157 (101%)	347 (99%)	84 (99%)	588 [99%]
Per cent of 588	(27%)	(59%)	(14%)	(100%)

Patients with stays of less than three years include most of the 63 men who were referred from prison and returned there after treatment and some of the 68 men who were referred from other hospitals and soon returned there. The total lack of association with diagnosis is surprising since in ordinary psychiatric hospitals most occupants of beds in any long stay wards would be chronic schizophrenics.

Table 3.3
Length of stay in Special Hospital by admission offence (N 588)

Offence	>3yrs	3 > 6 years	6+ years	Total
Homicide	31 (20%)	45 (28%)	82 (52%)	158 [27%]
Attempted homicide	22 (41%)	9 (17%)	23 (43%)	54 [9%]
Sexual	8 (17%)	8 (17%)	32 (67%)	48 [8%]
Arson	15 (28%)	25 (46%)	14 (25%)	54 [9%]
Assault	64 (35%)	59 (33%)	58 (32%)	181 [31%]
Acquisitive	17 (39%)	15 (34%)	12 (27%)	44 [7%]
Other	14 (29%)	18 (37%)	17 (35%)	49 [8%]
Total	171 (29%)	179 (30%)	238 (40%)	588 (100%)

x^2=47.52, df 12, p<.001; Cramer's V .28

Patients who committed homicide or a sexual offence were more likely to stay for longer than six years. Mean length of stay for sexual offenders was nine years; for men with an admission offence of homicide (or attempted homicide) it was eight years (or 7.5 years). These figures underestimate the average length of stay for men admitted directly from court because referrals from prison, who returned there quite quickly, are included. Since men committing homicide were more likely to be older on admission than other patients, see Table 3.4, they would be much older at departure than most other patients. They were also significantly more likely to stay in NHS hospitals longer than most other offenders, as were patients with an admission offence of attempted homicide.

Table 3.4
Admission offence by age on admission, above and below 30 (N 588)

Offence	30 and under	31 and over
Homicide	58 (37%)	100 (63%)
Att.homicide	31 (57%)	23 (43%)
Sexual offence	32 (67%)	16 (33%)
Arson	31 (57%)	23 (43%)
Assault	79 (40%)	102 (60%)
Acquisitive	28 (64%)	16 (36%)
Other	27 (55%)	22 (45%)

x^2=25.16, df 6, p<.001; Cramer's V .21

Admission offences were associated with the Restriction Orders described on page 6, see Table 3.5 opposite. Although admission offences were associated with both Restriction Orders (Table 3.5) and with lengths of stay in hospital (Table 3.3) there was no association between Restriction Orders and lengths of stay in hospital although doctors thought that such an order delayed discharge. 80 per cent of 'active' patients were restricted, see Table 3.6.

Table 3.5
'Restricted' by admission offence - active sample (N 330)
(Percentages were similar for the whole sample)

Offence	Restricted	Not restricted
Homicide (64 + 2) and		
attempted homicide (27 + 2)	91 (97%)	4 (3%)
Sexual	23 (70%)	10 (30%)
Arson	37 (93%)	3 (7%)
Assault *	77 (72%)	30 (28%)
Acquisitive	19 (68%)	9 (32%)
Other	18 (67%)	9 (33%)

* Of assaults on a police officer, only one was not restricted.

x^2=31.14, df 5, p<.001; Cramer's V .30: for whole sample, p<.001 and Cramer's V .33

Table 3.6
Was patient restricted at separation? (N 588/423/93/330)

	All 588	Core	Inactive	Active
Yes	450 [77%]	335 [79%]	70 [75%]	265 [80%]
No	138 [23%]	88 [21%]	23 [25%]	65 [20%]

The figures in Table 3.6. do not support the view that restrictions delay discharge from NHS hospitals: in that case there would have been a greater proportion of restricted patients amongst the 'inactive'. (Moreover, since some 'inactive' patients had only been transferred from the Special Hospital during the last few weeks of the research period and discharge for the 'restricted' could hardly have been effected in that time, a slightly higher proportion of restricted patients would be expected to be found amongst the 'inactive' if even minor delays caused by bureaucratic procedures slowed the return of restricted patients to the community). In fact the average length of stay for restricted patients in NHS hospitals was one year eight months, two months shorter than the average of one year ten months for unrestricted patients and there was no difference in the number of subsequent readmissions for the two groups.

Diagnosis was a major factor affecting the way in which patients returned to the community, see Table 3.7 overleaf in which, incidentally, it is possible to avoid statistical problems concerning

significance and small numbers by combining all transfers to custody
– SH and HMP; such a revision hardly affects the reported levels of
significance and association.

Table 3.7 shows that relatively few psychopaths were transferred to
NHS hospitals. 65 per cent of all psychopaths were discharged
directly into the community compared to 16 per cent of
schizophrenics. Fifteen psychopaths were being prescribed major
tranquillisers at the time of discharge and most of these were
amongst the transferred patients; and despite the reported
reluctance of hospitals to admit patients with this diagnosis,
another 16 had subsequent hospital admissions.

Table 3.7
Discharge mode (core sample) by major diagnoses – (N 362)

Discharge	Psychopathic	Schizophrenic
Conditional	62 (73%)	23 (27%)
Absolute	13 (45%)	16 (55%)
Transfer to NHS	29 (13%)	189 (87%)
Transfer to SH	8 (31%)	18 (69%)
Transfer to HMP	3 (75%)	1 (25%)
Total	115 (32%)	247 (68%)

X^2=106.51, df 4, p<.001; Cramer's V .49

There is a considerable body of opinion which would not accept a
diagnosis of psychopathy or personality disorder as an indication of
mental illness likely to respond to treatment. Nearly a fifth of the
173 doctors who were respondents in the study specifically stated
that the patient for whom they were formally responsible was not ill
and would not be receiving treatment if it were not for the legal
requirements of a Restriction Order. Nevertheless after leaving the
Special Hospital over a quarter of patients with a diagnosis of
psychopathy received medication or treatment in hospital. Moreover,
although most psychopaths probably did not need medical care,
psychopaths and schizophrenics were equally likely to need
rehabilitation after a long period in a closed institution.

Admission diagnoses of psychopathy therefore had considerable
consequences for patients at the point of discharge (and, it will be
seen later, in their subsequent careers). However, it was apparent
from examination of case histories that admission diagnoses were
often made under difficulties. The strong association found between
diagnoses and preadmission histories, see Table 3.8, suggests that
diagnoses were much influenced by case histories, and these are known
to predispose the reader to interpret past behaviour as manifesting
criminality or illness (Cicourel, 1968; Garfinkel, 1967).

Table 3.8
Preadmission history by major diagnoses (N 503)

Preadmission	Psychopathic	Schizophrenic
Court appearances + hospital admissions	56 (30%)	133 (70%)
Only court appearances	71 (58%)	52 (42%)
Only hospital admissions	13 (12%)	93 (88%)
Neither	17 (20%)	68 (80%)
Total	157 (31%)	346 (69%)

X^2=63.19, df 3, p<.001; Cramer's V .35

Another factor strongly associated with diagnosis was ethnicity, black and brown patients being almost universally diagnosed as schizophrenics; their careers differed in a number of ways from other patients however and these findings will be discussed later. Admission offence was associated with diagnosis, see Table 3.9, though less strongly than preadmission history. (Minor discrepancies in totals between tables result from the omission of individuals for whom any of the named variables were not known).

Table 3.9
Admission offence by major diagnoses (N 504)

Offence	Psych.	Schiz.
Homicide	29 (23%)	95 (77%)
Att.homicide	13 (28%)	34 (72%)
Sexual	25 (61%)	16 (39%)
Arson	26 (52%)	24 (48%)
Assault	40 (25%)	120 (75%)
Acquisitive	12 (32%)	25 (68%)
Other	12 (27%)	33 (73%)
Total	157 (31%)	347 (69%)

X^2=34.29, df 6, p<.001; Cramer's V .26

Age was also associated with diagnosis, see Table 3.10 overleaf, young patients being more likely to be diagnosed as psychopathic, particularly if they also had criminal histories. Older patients were more likely to be diagnosed as schizophrenic, especially if they had had admissions to a psychiatric hospital. There is a strong link between youth and criminal activity in all criminal statistics, but it is also probable that deviant behaviour perceived as criminal in a young man may be seen as more inappropriate in an older man, who may then be referred for medical treatment.

Table 3.10
Admission age by major diagnoses (N 504)

	30 and under	31 and over
Psychopathic	116 [45%]	41 [17%]
Schizophrenic	141 [55%]	206 [83%]
Total	257 (51%)	247 (49%)

x^2=47.82, df 1, p<.001; phi .31

The associations found between age, admission offence and preadmission history, coupled with the evidence of subsequent medical treatment of some psychopaths, support an argument that some young men diagnosed as psychopaths were embryonic schizophrenics who, had they spent more time in the community, might have had the hospital admissions which were so strongly related to an admission diagnosis of schizophrenia. Indeed, given the age, admission offence, ethnicity and preadmission history of a patient it is possible to predict diagnosis with a very small margin of error, though the factor most strongly associated with diagnosis for the majority of patients was preadmission history based on case histories.

Environments to which patients where discharged

Hospitals

This was the placement recommended by the Butler and Aarvold Committees and 44 per cent of all patients were 'separated' by transfer to NHS hospitals. Of the small proportion who remained 'inactive' in these hospitals most were elderly and schizophrenic; only 13 psychopathic patients stayed in NHS hospitals for more than a year. Black and brown patients, however, although predominantly diagnosed as schizophrenic, very rarely remained 'inactive', a finding discussed in more detail in Chapter Four.

A quarter of all NHS hospital doctors interviewed said that Special Hospital patients did not differ in any way from their other patients. Two fifths of all patients were reported to differ but in an unexpected way. They were said to be 'a pleasure to look after', or they were 'perfect gentlemen' with 'exemplary behaviour'. Sometimes this approval was tempered by concern over possible institutionalisation. Indeed, a further 27 patients in NHS hospitals were described as 'submissive', 'over willing to please', 'pathetic', and 'socially incompetent' and there were frequent references to the problems this created for rehabilitation. Only ten inpatients were, it has already been reported in Chapter Two, seriously troublesome, and four of these were recalled.

Of patients who left the hospitals, a quarter did so within six months, half had left within a year, 80 per cent within two years. Patients whose offence had involved wives and siblings as victims were significantly more likely to stay longer. The average length of stay in NHS hospitals for those whose admission offence was homicide or attempted homicide was two years, and for sexual offenders, one year and six months, but the range was very wide, some patients in each of these categories leaving within two months. A stay of one or two years seemed very long to NHS doctors who were used to a much more rapid turnover of patients. It was a shorter time than had been anticipated by Special Hospital doctors who envisaged 'stability in an institution' as the final disposition of most transferred patients.

There were obvious differences between hospitals. Those in urban areas were apparently under more pressure to discharge patients in order to free beds for more urgent admissions than those in many rural areas. Patients in urban hospitals were also more easily able to become accustomed to the world outside the hospital than patients in some remote rural areas who depended on staff understanding, transport and initiative to become better integrated. One patient remained, apparently content, in a hospital where staff erroneously thought he could not be discharged without some initiative from the Home Office. In another hospital a door marked 'Rehabilitation Unit' led to an unused room. In many hospitals there were carefully planned stages in rehabilitation through various wards and group homes and hostels generally designed for patients whose progress was anticipated to be leisurely and who when they arrived at the final stage were unlikely to proceed further. Frustration was mentioned by patients (and supervisors) when for reasons other than those of health it was impossible to obtain permission for discharge into the community for Special Hospital patients who made rapid progress and quickly completed all stages of rehabilitation.

Other environments

Other environments to which patients were discharged, either directly from the Special Hospital or after a stay in an NHS hospital, included hostels and private accommodation. Family circumstances had changed for patients whose stays had been lengthy. Parents were older, some had died or become old and frail. Still, 39 per cent of men under thirty were discharged to live with parents, although only half as many over thirty years of age could be accommodated in this way. Half the married men were divorced, but almost all the wives of those who remained married offered them homes when they returned to the community.

Special Hospital doctors viewed family interest with mixed feelings, especially where a member of the family had been a victim of the admission offence. 'It is not Special Hospital policy to return attempted matricides to their mothers or patients with morbid jealousy to their spouses'. For this reason, and perhaps because of the work of authorities such as Leff (1982), Laing and Esterson (1964) and Cooper (1971), all of whom regarded the family as a contributory factor in relapse, a hostel placement was frequently preferred. Close relatives who looked after patients were likely to have had little information from or contact with Special Hospital consultants and 26 per cent of doctors responsible for patients in the community did not know the patient's family; a further 14 per cent knew about them only at second hand. The role of the family is discussed more fully in Chapter Five.

Overall, first accommodation was found for just under half of all patients by social workers, usually those working in hospitals, and for a similar proportion by the patient's family or friends, only a few patients being able to provide their own housing.

By the end of the research period over a third of patients had found their own accommodation, just under a third still being housed by family or friends and only seven per cent still being in accommodation found by hospital staff. 16 per cent were in accommodation found by other social workers or probation officers.

A similar shift towards independence is shown in Tables 3.11 below and 3.12 opposite which also show that the situation of patients in the community was not dissimilar from that at entry, except that those homeless on admission were almost all settled in accommodation; and most of those who had left their parents had done so to live with wives. Percentages are for an average of 288 patients in each column (none less than 200) since the tables omit patients living in hospitals or in prison for some time before admission, or those for whom the listed postdischarge information was missing.

Table 3.11
Accommodation at admission and after discharge (percentages)

Type of accommodation	At admission	After discharge First	Latest
Owner occupied	18%	16%	16%
Council rented	33%	26%	40%
Private rented	16%	9%	19%
Lodgings	14%	10%	15%
Hostel	6%	39%	9%
No fixed abode	13%	1%	1%

About a quarter of all these patients had difficulties in finding accommodation. A small proportion changed their accommodation frequently, but most remained in the same accommodation or changed only once or twice to improve their situation or to join wives and families.

Nine per cent of patients were asked to leave their first accommodation because of their behaviour (and were then most likely to return to close relatives) but two-thirds had been in their latest accommodation more than a year at the date of interview.

Table 3.12
With whom living at admission and after discharge (percentages)

Description	At admission	After discharge First	Latest
Wife	26%	11%	31%
Alone	31%	8%	30%
Parents	35%	28%	12%
Siblings	2%	6%	3%
Friends	3%	3%	4%
Hostel residents, other relatives,etc.	3%	44%	21%

It was interesting to find that of 16 active patients whose wives had been the victims of their admission offences, five had remarried or were cohabiting at the time of interview, four having married within a year of discharge. Of 14 active patients whose victim had been a child, one had become a father and three were cohabiting with women whose children formed part of the household. (This data excludes temporary liaisons).

Hostels

Although doctors preferred hostel placements when hospital places were not available, only a third of patients who had been hostel residents felt at home there and most hostels expected residents to move on after a few months. Of 112 patients discharged to hostels, only 15 were accommodated in group homes which catered for chronic patients who were expected to stay for long periods. Of these 15, only five remained in a group home at the end of the research period and two of those were still technically inpatients since the home belonged to a hospital. Only 18 patients stayed in a hostel for two or more years and over a third had moved by the end of six months, 65 per cent by the end of a year. Patients and their supervisors commented adversely upon the standard of accommodation and administration in some hostels; one or two were notoriously badly managed but were thought to be the only possible placement for a patient returning to an area where no hospital would accept him; and some hostels for psychiatric patients were primarily for the mentally handicapped and unsuitable for these Broadmoor patients. After years of institutional life some patients found the intimacy of even well run hostel life uncongenial and were eager to leave and live alone.

Some hostels run on therapeutic community lines were stressful for patients who had expected to put therapy behind them.

If rehabilitation in a hospital was not available, hostels were rarely more than a temporary refuge and in Chapter Five some evidence of association between hostel placement and relapse will be discussed. Families were likely to be the main support of patients in the community unless the patient preferred to live alone.

Living alone

Some supervisors reported a guilty concern about what they perceived as the 'isolation' of patients living in single accommodation. However, the patients appeared content and most did not think themselves lonely. Some were resistant to being pressed into attendance at clubs and a recorded fall off in rates of such attendance may represent increasing independence from social work efforts to incorporate patients into an artificial social atmosphere. An analysis of changes in the frequency and type of patients' social contacts between the period just after discharge and the time of interview suggested a shift to domesticity and less dependence on casual drinking contacts rather than a withdrawn existence for most patients. It was not demonstrable that isolation was more common amongst patients than amongst the general population; many had a very active social life. Almost half the single patients married, half within a year of discharge, hardly suggesting that a Special Hospital background inhibited social contact.

Homosexual relationships were probably common in Broadmoor and it is possible that as a result some patients may have found difficulty in reestablishing their sexual life. Of 18 patients known to have had homosexual affairs whilst in Broadmoor seven were reported to have had difficulties subsequently, four in establishing stable heterosexual relationships, two in establishing stable homosexual relationships and one, very young on admission to Broadmoor, in establishing a clear sexual identity. Twenty patients in all experienced problems in establishing sexual relationships and thirteen of these had difficulties over sexual identity.

Employment

Some patients and some supervisors thought that discharge could not be effected until employment had been obtained; other supervisors thought it unwise to discharge a man without some occupation, especially if he had a history of drink or other problems.

A satisfactory rate of employment was achieved, when all factors are considered. At the time of interview 42 per cent of patients were employed in the open market in competition with others seeking work, 13 per cent in sheltered employment. If the 16 per cent of active patients who were disabled are discounted, there was a net shift of five per cent towards a less satisfactory employment pattern than that recorded for patients when admitted. This may reflect the general increase in the rate of unemployment since most patients were admitted.

However, when the difficulties with which patients contended are considered, their level of employment seems praiseworthy. Many had spent long periods in hospital, or had several hospital admissions. Moreover, it was noticeable that patients who were unable to complete interviews or grids because of the effects of medication were not reported by their supervisors to be disabled, although the situation must have affected their prospects of work. 27 per cent of patients interviewed complained about the side effects of medication and if these patients are regarded as disabled, the employment record for patients is better than that prior to admission, despite increasing unemployment in the country.

It had been thought that rapid changes of employment might indicate patient instability but first jobs were often unsatisfactory and rapid changes almost always led to improvement and stable employment. 78 per cent of those working found employment within six months of leaving hospital and most found their own jobs. These were very often temporary and a third of those so employed lost their first job through no fault of their own. A third were still in their first job and the remainder mostly left to obtain better pay or conditions, only a handful being dismissed for poor time keeping, quarrelling with workmates, etc. Some patients went to extraordinary lengths to obtain and keep jobs. Occasionally, because of problems and delays in obtaining benefits to which they were entitled, they walked miles to and from work waiting for pay day; or walked similar distances during transport strikes; or went without food to afford tools or fares. Some were manifestly exploited by employers, occasionally by relatives, who realised how difficult it was for patients to obtain employment.

Supervisors and patients thought that disclosure of Special Hospital background reduced employment prospects (a third of all patients interviewed considered that problems in obtaining work were related to their Special Hospital background). Only 41 per cent of current employers knew the Special Hospital background of patients compared to 74 per cent of first employers. The effects of disclosure and employment upon reintegration are discussed in Chapter Five.

Several patients found it very difficult to accept that they would never be able to return to their original employment. Sometimes it was hard to understand why return was discouraged by their supervisors. Some supervisors seemed to be able to cope with patients whose jobs, for example, took them all over the country and abroad; others, occasionally because they misunderstood the implication of the Restriction Order, would not allow their clients to take jobs if this meant a change of address. Some public bodies or large firms would not employ patients if the work entailed calling on members of the public. Some patients then took up similar work as a form of private enterprise. Because of problems concerning receipt of benefit supervisors were not always informed about this, or they turned a blind eye to the situation.

Occupational skills

Occupations before admission and after discharge were similar, with a fractional shift from unskilled to skilled employment. This reflects the greater opportunities for employment for patients with skills, however rusty, and is not attributable to any training which patients received.

Training in trades and skills in the Special Hospital was primarily therapeutic and one or two patients were disappointed to find that skills acquired there were unmarketable. Only nine per cent of patients had subsequently attended government sponsored employment training courses. Six per cent of active patients had applied for assessment or training unsuccessfully. Many patients were critical of the Disablement Resettlement Service. Officers were sometimes thought to be unhelpful because of the stigma of the Special Hospital background or because the service was mainly interested in physically disabled people. (There was corroborating evidence that one or two patients were unable to proceed with training or retraining because of difficulties due to stigma which prevented them obtaining accommodation during a course). However, only seven of those who had had training were using this at the date of interview and most of these had paid for their training or it had been paid for by friends, relatives or employers. Patients' advice to those newly discharged was to avoid training schemes but to take any kind of employment, however unsatisfactory, in order to obtain national insurance records and references.

Social skills

21 per cent of active patients had had some kind of social skills training, a rather low percentage considering expectations of postdischarge rehabilitation. The problem most frequently mentioned by patients, after that of finding employment, was the difficulty of adapting to the world outside the Special Hospital. Specific examples which recurred included fear of traffic which was now faster and denser, and fear of crowds. Those who could drive had to relearn traffic signs and regulations. More than one walked miles because of

an inability to cope with buses where the passenger had to pay on entry. Embarrassment resulted from changes in customs in public houses, where requests for beer phrased in terms appropriate seven years earlier were met with blank stares or sarcasm. All these problems were exacerbated by the patient's nervousness that his ignorance would disclose his background or land him in trouble. Supermarket shopping presented difficulties for patients admitted before these were common and some mentioned their fear of being accused of shoplifting because of their unfamiliarity with new modes of shopping. Patients also encountered difficulties with decimal coinage, with unfamiliar shapes of coins and sizes of paper money. Metrication presented a particular problem for skilled or semiskilled tradesmen who found they had to contend with different sized tools (and many more power driven tools) as well as novel and differently sized materials. Setting up home from scratch with little or no financial aid presented very considerable problems, especially to men who had been cared for by wives and mothers before admission, and who were also amazed and disconcerted at the way costs of basic items such as cleaning materials, soap, lighting and heating (and cooking utensils and ingredients if they managed to cater for themselves) had risen.

Patients reported a lack of understanding of and training in the kinds of skills they most needed, particularly in relating to women and in understanding changed mores about women and sex; in registering for various kinds of benefit or with a family doctor (ten per cent were known not to be registered with a family doctor at the date of interview and five per cent reported difficulties - nine had been refused); and in dealing with practical problems already mentioned. Some thought that an introduction to the outside world whilst they were still in Broadmoor would have been helpful; others would have preferred a period of training immediately after their departure though some patients commented that the supervisors whom they encountered at this stage were not trained for such work. Patients whom supervisors thought not 'ill' and apparently intelligent and selfsufficient found it difficult to ask for assistance; they probably needed exceptionally tactful handling and supervisors may have been unaware of their need. On the other hand some social supervisors took on almost a fulltime occupation with patients who were perceived to have been ill, to need a great deal of this kind of assistance, and who readily accepted help.

Financial problems

Two-fifths of active patients were known to have financial problems and a third of those interviewed had had difficulties over welfare benefits. Two thirds of all these problems were resolved with the assistance of the social supervisor. About a fifth reported having had a resettlement grant, a form of benefit with which social

33

supervisors were often unfamiliar. Patients were more likely to hear about these grants from fellow patients or hospital staff and the amount of benefit varied greatly. Some had a few pounds, some a very substantial sum for setting themselves up with equipment or tools for work. Some were unwittingly disqualified because they had spent a long time in hospital waiting for accommodation and had been earning (often a pittance) during that time. Some misunderstood the situation and expected a handout from a small fund kept for emergencies at Broadmoor. Almost all said they had had great difficulties in managing money, either because of inflation or because of changes in coinage.

Some patients commented that staff at the social security offices were unhelpful and that it was embarrassing to have to make disclosure of background to clerical staff, but the majority of complaints about welfare benefits concerned underpayment and late arrival of benefit. Some patients were reported by their social supervisors to be living in penury for weeks whilst their affairs were sorted out, having only a few pence to manage with after paying rent; one of those who was in trouble soon after discharge had made a scene at the social security office which his social supervisor thought not entirely unjustified.

Vulnerability

Several patients described their vulnerability when, for example, there were thefts or other offences in workplaces, or their alarm if they were in hostels where they might become involved in minor criminal activities (by unwittingly handling goods pilfered from their places of employment by other residents, for example). Some were harrassed by workmates and neighbours (one had had his flat broken into and his property stolen more than once) who perceived that the patient would be reluctant to draw attention to himself by complaining to the police. Social supervisors volunteered corroborating statements in a number of these cases.

55 per cent of active patients were contacted by the police, usually when a crime had been committed in the area, and 79 charges were brought as a result of a quarter of these contacts. Of these charges six were dismissed and six were relatively minor traffic offences. Seven per cent of patients were contacted five or more times, 26 per cent more than three times and patients often found this upsetting. Black and brown patients were particularly likely to be contacted by the police and charged as a result and the evidence for this will be discussed in Chapter Four.

Supervision

The relationship between different types of supervision and success in the community will be discussed in Chapter Five, but some account of the supervision experienced by patients may help to put this aspect of post discharge careers into perspective.

'Formal' supervisions were statutorily undertaken in accordance with a condition of a Restriction Order, or occasionally as the result of a subsequent Court Order and could only be lapsed at the discretion of the supervisor or ended with the agreement of the Home Secretary unless a date for termination had been prescribed by the Court. Other 'informal' supervisions were engaged in voluntarily by both supervisor and patient, either of whom could elect to end the relationship. Some patients continued to have informal supervision after being absolutely discharged from the condition of a Restriction Order which required formal supervision.

69 patients had 'leave' from the Special Hospital (occasionally on trial to an NHS hospital) and 102 patients had leave from an NHS hospital before discharge. Another nine had leave from both kinds of hospital before discharge. Their hospital doctors continued to be formally responsible for them and usually, but not always, arranged for supervision by a social worker or probation officer; sometimes nurses supervised the patient or there might be no regular supervision. When efficiently organised, supervised leave was a useful way of ensuring that patients who were about to be absolutely discharged had some assistance when first in the community and nursing staff often provided an admirable link between hospital and community. However, because a patient on leave was still technically an inpatient, problems over welfare benefits sometimes arose, especially if employment was obtained, with which only experienced social workers or probation officers would have been qualified to deal. In addition, when leave for a restricted patient was not well supervised misunderstandings could occur when formal discharge was eventually effected whilst he remained in the community. A patient might then resent the fact that he was for the first time expected to make regular appointments with newly appointed supervisors.

Other problems arose when individual supervisors made arrangements for supervision to be shared. Some Special Hospital doctors retained nominal formal supervision but delegated practical supervision to a colleague in the community, an arrangement which other NHS doctors found unacceptable. Some transferred formal supervision but retained an advisory role. The original partners to such an agreement and the first social supervisor of any conditionally discharged patient were usually (but not always) well informed about their statutory responsibilities, since the Home Office provided notes about these and also asked the psychiatrist to give the social supervisor an adequate briefing about the patient's medical history. However, when staff changed, moved or retired, their successors were often less well informed and in a few cases totally unaware of their statutory obligations. In most cases the Home Office would become aware of a complete breakdown in supervision when the usual quarterly reports ceased to arrive. However, in cases where supervisors were known to be extremely tardy in supplying reports or adamantly refused to do so, some supervisions effectively lapsed when a supervisor moved or retired and this situation would remain undisclosed unless a crisis occurred. Sometimes a similar lapse occurred (or supervisors had only a hazy understanding of the responsibilities and conditions of formal supervision) when shared or other supervisions had been inherited and earlier notes on statutory responsibilities or understandings about shared responsibility had been mislaid or remained unread. Other problems also occurred and the adverse consequences of these for patients will be described in Chapter Five.

In any case, the majority of formal supervisions did not last very long. 47 per cent of formal social supervisions had ceased by the end of two years after separation, 77 per cent by four years. Half of formal medical supervisions had ceased before absolute discharge and before the end of the third year after separation, 75 per cent before four years. Almost all of these had ceased on the recommendation of the supervisor with the approval of the Home Office. 36 per cent of 47 absolute discharges and 46 per cent of all 60 'effective' absolute discharges occurred in the first two years after separation. (Thirteen patients were 'effectively' absolutely discharged after a lengthy spell of leave in the community during which they had had full supervision, treated in this study as if it had been 'formal'). 72 patients had had some informal medical supervision, 40 from the date they left Broadmoor, but this lapsed quite quickly, for almost a third within three months, 73 per cent by the end of 12 months, and all but three within three years. Although two-fifths of doctors approved of supervision lasting for at least five years (eight thought that it should last for a lifetime), four-fifths of absolute discharges occurred before the end of the fourth year after separation.

Medical supervision

Few doctors had comprehensive experience of the whole range of categories of patients, and some psychiatrists operated selection criteria which ensured that their experience was restricted. For example, some would not accept patients who had been diagnosed as psychopathic or any patients who were subject to restrictions. 88 per cent had only one or two patients in the sample in their care. Only eight per cent had had more than four cases in their care. Three of these were Special Hospital doctors of whom two have since retired. Ten NHS doctors supervised four or more members of the sample (and may in addition have supervised patients from other Special Hospitals).

In addition to the practice of delegating practical responsibility to another consultant, a further obvious difference between supervision by Special Hospital doctors and NHS doctors was that the former, having no regular outpatient clinic, rarely saw patients nominally in their care unless some crisis occurred. Supervision in some instances was extremely tenuous, ten cases having effectively lapsed.

Patients mostly had a stable relationship with their psychiatrist, 70 per cent having no change of doctor and a total of over 90 per cent having only one or two changes, though some had as many as 15. The majority of patients always saw the supervising consultant, some doctors specifically stating that this was to spare the patient the painful necessity of repeating his past history. About a fifth were seen by registrars, sometimes by a series of registrars. Less than half these patients complained but their supervision sometimes seemed to suffer. For example, although one patient was thought to be on medication, no records of the type or dosage could be found by the registrar responsible; it transpired that the patient was obtaining repeated prescriptions from his family doctor. In fact 22 per cent of all patients on medication obtained this from the family doctor and it was regretted that no approach had been made to the appropriate professional association at the outset of the study in order to encourage cooperation. No responses were received from any family doctors, known to be prescribing for patients, to whom individual approaches were made late in the study when no other doctor was involved.

Doctors interviewed expressed dissatisfaction with the supervision of Special Hospital patients on two main grounds. Firstly, because of patients' characteristics, though it has already been reported this was rarely because patients were overtly dangerous or difficult. Nearly a quarter said that the patients for whom they were responsible were not ill and would not have been in treatment if this had not been a condition of the warrant of discharge. Patients supervised by another seven doctors did not progress and were reluctant to engage in any therapeutic interaction. In all these cases doctors were manifestly ill at ease in an unusual relationship where a patient was constrained to accept treatment which either he or the doctor thought unnecessary. Doctors also reported that patients were stigmatised by their Special Hospital history, which made nursing staff 'hostile', 'anxious' and 'over sensitive to the slightest misdemeanour'. Since a fifth of doctors interviewed expressed anxieties about possible but not actual repetition of deviant behaviour by the patient for whom they were responsible it seems possible that some doctors were similarly affected.

The second main ground for dissatisfaction with supervision stemmed from the bureaucratic control to which a restricted patient and his supervisor were subject. Only a quarter of doctors thought that the Home Secretary or his Department had a responsibility for patients which equalled or was greater than their own. A third of all comments made by doctors criticised the way responsibility was exercised by the Home Office. 34 doctors mentioned dissatisfaction with what they perceived as lay intervention in clinical matters; disagreements, which probably arose from conflicts between the Home Office statutory responsibility for public safety and doctors' concern for individual patients, may have led doctors to assume that their clinical judgements were in question. Sometimes complaints were due to misplaced expectations about the role of the Home Office and there was evidence of confusion and misunderstanding about some issues concerning restricted patients. A number of doctors were unaware that their initiative was required to recommend termination or lapsing of supervision, or reduction in the frequency of contacts or reports.

Psychiatrists are accustomed to dealing with individuals face to face and several expressed dislike of bureaucratic methods, having to write to or telephone faceless individuals whose status they could not readily ascertain. Those with most experience generally (though not always) found contact with the Home Office satisfactory and some doctors managed to negotiate the system to the advantage of their patients; it was the majority with little experience who found the situation most problematic. However, 60 per cent of complaints concerned bureaucratic delays. (The Home Office commented that it was considering means by which to improve the standard of service in its dealings with supervisors). The uneasy relationships with patients which doctors reported stemmed at least in some instances from a lack of knowledge of how to negotiate Home Office consent to reductions in contact with apparently well outpatients or to long leave for similar inpatients. A combination of unease, anxiety and irritation caused by delays in Home Office response to correspondence may have contributed to the illusion (see page 23) that restricted patients stayed longer in hospital than the unrestricted.

There were also some confusions about the role of the Department of Health and Social Security in relation to patients but most doctors thought the Department's responsibility was confined to providing facilities and requested more and improved resources. Some doctors thought that the Department should overrule local or regional administration to ensure that places were readily available in Special Hospitals when recall was recommended, that placements were available in all NHS hospitals, and that full and not partial details about transferred patients were available to doctors involved in supervision in the community. Conflicts between disclosure and confidentiality are discussed later.

Only 26 per cent of NHS doctors (but almost all Special Hospital doctors) chose their social supervising colleague. Such choice may be critical in ensuring effective collaboration, since 12 per cent mentioned the overriding importance of personality when expressing preferences for particular agencies. However, 60 per cent of doctors preferred to collaborate with probation officers. Doctors expressed criticism of local authority based social workers (though rarely of hospital social workers) four times as often as probation officers, whom they perceived as older, more experienced, more professional and better trained. Doctors were correct, according to the data, in thinking that probation officers who supervised Special Hospital patients were significantly more likely to be older than social workers but incorrect in thinking that social workers were more often unqualified, had fewer years of service or were less stable in post. In fact hospital social workers, with whom most doctors preferred to work, were found to be significantly (p<.05) more likely to move than any other kind of social supervisor. Probation Service areas are large and officers are therefore more likely to be able to continue supervision if a patient moves to a new address, but local authority social workers whose 'patches' were smaller were equally stable in post. Also, although they were significantly (p<.01) younger than the probation officers, only 40 per cent of social workers supervising patients were under 35, compared to 47 per cent in a national sample (Association of Directors of Social Services, 1981) and 34 per cent were over 45, compared to 29 per cent in the national sample, so there seems to have been some deliberate choice of mature workers for this task.

Social workers not based in hospitals were described by some doctors as 'unrealistic', 'marxist', 'the left wing bearded brigade'. Amongst 56 reasons given for negative attitudes were that social workers 'questioned diagnoses', 'challenged Sections', were difficult for doctors to 'control', 'act like community workers' (although occasionally said to be 'more interested in interpersonal relationships than practical help') or queried aspects of medical supervision.

The Department of Health and Social Security discussion document on community care (DHSS, 1978) suggested that some misunderstandings between social workers and doctors arise from differing expectations which result from training nonmedical social workers to assist clients to make decisions for themselves while training doctors to make decisions for patients. This might account for doctors' more favourable perception of their relationship with the Probation Service, members of which have controlling functions as 'officers of the court'. Social workers, however, also have statutory obligations, for example in child care, but this was one reason why a few doctors found them 'troublesome'. If a patient returned to a household including children, the local Social Service team often expected the supervising doctor to concern himself with the welfare of the whole family unit; this expectation irritated some doctors, one of whom said 'It is not my job to relieve the anxieties of his family, I am here to treat the patient'. Doctors generally found the collaborative relationship easier when the statutory obligations of the social supervisor coincided with medical traditions, focussing upon the individual.

The Probation Service may also be more acceptable to doctors since it does not make claims to knowledge about mental health. Medical social workers and nurses (according to studies reviewed by Huntingdon, 1981) generally defer to medical opinion about patients in the community. Doctors, rarely trained in the skills required to rehabilitate patients in the community, may be ruffled by bids for professional autonomy from other workers in the area of community mental health. An anecdote, frequently retailed with minor variations by doctors in different parts of the country, described the eventual humiliation of a social worker who challenged medical opinion on the strength of specialist mental health social work training. This seemed to be an 'atrocity story' akin to those told by other professionals about doctors and cited by Huntingdon as symbolising frustration and friction in the jostling for power in the field of community medicine.

Social supervision

Social supervisors were conscientious in their supervision of patients, seeing them regularly and reporting to and initiating contacts with their doctors (and occasionally, in desperation, with the Home Office when doctors did not respond). Analysis of repertory grids (see Table 5.1A in Chapter Five) showed that a quarter of all patients would choose a social supervisor as their preferred helper, although individual social supervisors were rarely of great importance to patients (see Table 5.2 also in Chapter Five) probably because they changed so frequently.

Social supervisors in all agencies moved, sometimes to work for another agency, sometimes on transfer by promotion or to different duties. More than half of 295 patients had two or more supervisors, ten per cent had four or more supervisors. Periods of supervision by the same supervisor usually lasted less than two years and 20 per cent lasted less than six months. Patients particularly disliked having to recall their past history when supervisors changed. Although social workers were more stable in post than doctors generally assumed and patients rarely saw a substitute for the social supervisor currently responsible, there was evidence of a lack of continuity of care which, it will be argued later, was detrimental.

Other problems arose because supervisors lacked a clear idea of their role, a limitation perceived by those patients who expressed a need for specialist rehabilitation. In addition, since this was usually their first experience of such patients, supervisors were, as suggested on page 14, at a loss when endeavouring to assess progress. Only ten supervisors had specific training for work in the field of mental health and all but one of these were social workers. It was also often the case, according to supervisors interviewed, that senior social workers or probation officers from whom fieldworkers expected support and advice had similarly limited experience of such supervision; or in rare cases where this was not so, the patients were so different that earlier experience was not helpful. This was partly because of the changes in characteristics of discharged patients during recent decades, briefly mentioned in Chapter One and discussed in detail in Chapter Six.

Supervisors' expectations about the way in which responsibility was shared varied in a confusing manner. Doctors and social supervisors were equally divided, a third of each group thinking responsibility was equally shared, another third thinking the doctor was chiefly responsible and a third that the social supervisor had the greater responsibility. However, the perceptions of doctor and social supervisor only coincided in 19 per cent of situations where agreement could be tested. Some recognition of the fact that opinions and practices vary and of the consequent necessity for explicit negotiation, at the outset of collaborative supervision, of the way in which responsibility is to be shared might reduce opportunities for misunderstandings.

Social supervisors were handicapped in some instances by inadequate information about the patient. 25 per cent of social supervisors reported not having received a sociomedical history (or the equivalent in the form of letters, detailed discussions, or having access to such a history), although doctors reported having made such histories available to all but six per cent of social supervisors. Reported receipt of such information varied significantly between agencies. 89 per cent of hospital social workers had access to sociomedical histories although some NHS doctors themselves did not have full details of patients' histories; 75 per cent of probation officers and 59 per cent of local authority based social workers had such information.

Nonreceipt of histories may be partly due to changes of personnel since although only five per cent of doctors disapproved of giving such information to social supervisors many doctors stated that they were selective in practice, saying for example, 'it depends on my view of the individual social worker'. Although the Home Office asked the responsible doctor to send a sociomedical history to the social supervisor it was not clear that social supervisors were advised that this was something to which they had a reasonable entitlement or that the Home Office would assist if the doctor disagreed. Patients when leaving the Special Hospital are often asked for their consent for such details to be given to social supervisors, an agreement probably made under technical duress, although if supervision is a condition of discharge the ethical situation is confusing. A patient has a right to refuse but this was never mentioned as a reason for not giving information to a social supervisor. It is true that patients were sometimes discharged many years after bizarre events perhaps better forgotten; on the other hand there were a number of complaints by supervisors that their client was, unknown to them, in a situation where he was at risk which might have been avoided if fuller details of his background had been available. These were sometimes informal supervisions where ethical problems concerning disclosure and patient consent become even more complex.

It does seem unsatisfactory that a quarter of patients in the community were being supervised by social workers or probation officers with only a superficial knowledge of the patient's medical history. Such lack of knowledge often led to anxiety and failure of confidence. To overcome the ethical dilemma it might be good practice for social supervisors to ask their client (when there is no medical history on file) for written permission to apply for some information at the outset of supervision, that is before any sinister implication can be read into such a request. Further permission to hand on the information to a successor would avoid the patient's embarrassment when having to recapitulate his history for a new supervisor.

Only 44 per cent of social supervisors received copies of the doctor's quarterly report to the Home Office about restricted patients. There were differences between agencies similar to those reported for access to sociomedical histories. 67 per cent of hospital social workers, 41 per cent of local authority based social workers and 32 per cent of probation officers had access to doctors' quarterly reports. The formal or informal nature of supervision made no difference to this or any other aspect of collaboration. 80 per cent of doctors reported receiving copies of social supervisors' reports, including reports from some who were informally supervising and under no obligation to engage in this exercise. Communication about progress, bearing in mind that two-thirds of doctors thought their social supervising colleague had equal or greater responsibility, especially for reporting signs of relapse, did seem a little onesided.

Disclosure of background

The association between disclosure of background and patient success is discussed in Chapter Four. About two-fifths of doctors disapproved in principle of disclosing patients' Special Hospital background and only a third approved. However, when pressed to discuss specific situations, half of all doctors approved of disclosure to employers, landlords, prospective spouses or cohabitees. In practice disclosure also varied according to the recipient of the information, that is it depended on the doctor's assessment of individual personality or his view of agency confidentiality. In certain circumstances, because of hospital links with sources of accommodation and employment (for example, the local Disablement Resettlement Officer) disclosure to employers and landladies, etc. was almost inevitable. About half of doctors who approved of disclosure would only disclose with the permission of the patient. However, only a small proportion of doctors would intervene if the patient did not disclose; more would do so if the disclosure was to be made to an employer or landlord than to a prospective wife or cohabitee. Disclosure was thought to prejudice patient chances of obtaining employment and some doctors thought that requirements for disclosure to employers led patients to become self employed as windowcleaners, gardeners, etc., not always a desirable solution. The nature of the admission offence did not affect doctors' responses.

About a third of the doctors who approved of disclosure in principle said they left the practical implementation of this to the social worker, or occasionally to the patient. However, social supervisors were less likely than doctors to approve of disclosure, though only significantly so ($p < .005$) in the case of landlords. Social supervisors were in fact significantly more likely to approve of disclosure to wives ($p < .001$) than to either landlords or employers. Overt and occasionally bitter disagreements between supervisors about disclosure did sometimes occur but the opportunity for disagreements to be covert were common.

12 per cent of patients thought that some of their problems would have been avoided if they had not been required to disclose their history. Some patients were required by their supervisors to disclose to all employers or landlords and a few were required to give detailed accounts of their past offences to prospective spouses or growing children. Patients sometimes married first and told their supervisors later to avoid embarrassing confrontations; but the wives of all patients in this study who married after discharge knew that their husbands had been in a Special Hospital. Sometimes an offence was common knowledge in the area but otherwise it seemed to be very much a matter of chance whether a patient was required by a supervisor to disclose details of offences or had a supervisor who considered that disclosure merely of a previous mental illness was adequate. Nearly a fifth worried about the possibility of their history being discovered.

Postdischarge psychiatric and criminal careers

Before moving on to the next chapter to look at specific factors which were associated with reintegration a brief overview of postdischarge histories and particularly of the events used to assess patient integration, see Chapter Two, might be helpful.

Postdischarge psychiatric histories

43 per cent of all core sample patients discharged as 'schizophrenic showing symptoms' were described as symptom free at the date of interview. No such changes were recorded for patients diagnosed as psychopathic or personality disordered, evidence of pessimistic views amongst community services about the prognoses for these patients. Such views are inconsistent with changes recorded during stays at Broadmoor, where more than half of patients admitted as psychopaths were discharged as symptom free (a change in diagnosis regarded with scepticism by some NHS doctors). This pessimism is also inconsistent with evidence concerning changes in psychopaths being treated in an NHS hospital (Norris, 1983a).

69 per cent of inactive and 48 per cent of active patients were, according to social supervisors, receiving major tranquillisers at the date of interview and nearly half complained of side effects. Doctors reported 83 per cent of the inactive and 41 per cent of the active as on major tranquillisers. 32 per cent of 151 patients for whom details were available sometimes refused medication, and another eight per cent always refused. In three-quarters of all cases of reported refusal this caused problems. Half these constant refusers were readmitted to hospital. In seven cases where information was obtained from all three respondents, a doctor reported prescribing medication but both patient and supervisor said no medication was being taken. Moreover, some doubt remained about the accuracy of information about a number of patients not known to be refusing medication. Some psychiatrists prescribed oral medication, a quarter of the patients on medication were obtaining their own prescriptions from their family doctor, and doctors interviewed reported that two-thirds of their patients missed appointments for injected medication, a quarter missing two-thirds of their appointments or more. The effects of cessation of medication are discussed in Chapter Four.

48 patients were recalled to the Special Hospital and 35 of these were still there when research ended. The commonest reason for recall was aggressive behaviour, 16 (34 per cent) of cases recalled. Ten patients were recalled because they committed another offence, two because they absconded, four because symptoms recurred and four were repatriated patients who reentered the country. Five recalled patients had ceased taking medication. Three of them had refused medication and for two patients doctors withdrew medication, but conclusions about causation should be deferred until the section on medication in Chapter Four has been read.

84 patients were readmitted to NHS hospitals, 36 formally, 83 per cent of these once only. 64 patients were admitted informally but 16 of those formally admitted had also had informal readmissions. The peak time for readmission was in the third year after separation, a different pattern from that anticipated as a result of Black's (1982)

study where most readmissions occurred in the first two years. Reasons for discrepancies resulting from differences in the patients studied are discussed in Chapter Six. However, research relying entirely upon official statistics may be distorted if no account is taken of delays in recording. Access was granted to official data to check possible readmissions of patients whom the research team were having difficulty in tracing; it transpired that in almost every case the research team had later data than that officially recorded. The effort made during this study to obtain and record accurate data almost up to the date of presentation would probably not be justified in normal usage of official data; however, findings that most relapse occurs in the earliest years of a follow up study which deals with recent discharges may be an artefact of rather slow collection of data.

30 patients had a family member admitted to a psychiatric hospital after discharge, usually a sibling or mother; and a very high proportion of wives had had psychiatric inpatient treatment, although this finding results from the fact that patients frequently married fellow patients (or occasionally staff) whom they met in hospitals.

Postdischarge criminal histories

112 patients (including three about whom information was rather scanty and who are omitted from some analyses) appeared in court after separation, 41 of them on more than one occasion. A third of these patients were in court within six months of separation. Offences were most often acquisitive (theft, larceny, burglary, fraud) or 'other' offences which were usually of a relatively trivial nature. Two of the 212 patients admitted for homicide or attempted homicide committed a similar offence after separation but whilst still in custody; four others committed similar offences - two murders, two attempted murders - during the lengthy follow up period (detailed comparisons of preadmission and postdischarge offences are made in Chapter Four, see for example Tables 4.23 and 4.24). 45 per cent of those who reoffended committed a further serious offence. 'Serious' offences were sometimes technical offences and not dangerous, and there was a trend throughout to reoffend in a less serious manner. Only nine per cent of those 552 patients who were separated from the Special Hospital other than by death committed a further serious offence and only 20 per cent were charged with any kind of offence during a lengthy follow up. It is difficult to make comparisons with other offender populations since it would be rare for so many first offenders to be in custody for such long periods (and a small percentage of these patients had not committed any offence) but this would certainly be a very low rate of recidivism for a penal institution where inmates of a similar age had committed similar offences. Patients in this study seemed to have better post discharge careers than the earlier cohort studied by Black (1982) or the American patients studied by Thornberry and Jacoby (1979) when

all other factors were taken into consideration. In Chapter Six findings from those two studies are compared with those reported for the present study.

42 patients, of whom 19 had been in prison before admission, went to prison for a futher offence after discharge. Those who had been in prison before were likely to receive long sentences, five were for life and ten were for more than three years.

Details of vulnerability to police contact were discussed on page 34. The tact with which police contacted patients varied from area to area and some patients found the experience upsetting. One patient never left his home at night for fear of being accused of a crime. There was, however, no evidence that restricted patients, whose addresses were known to the police, were contacted more often than unrestricted patients.

Summary

Patients, most of whom had a history of deviant behaviour, were mainly single and many had disorganised home backgrounds, a history of unemployment, drinking problems and physical disabilities. However, for a third the admission offence was their first. Lengths of stay in hospital were associated with admission offence rather than diagnosis but diagnosis was strongly associated with preadmission history. Patients' families eventually provided accommodation for about half of all patients, although placements in hospital or hostels were generally thought preferable by doctors. A satisfactory rate of employment was achieved by patients despite various handicaps, and a shift towards independence was recorded despite lack of social skills, financial problems and vulnerabilities.

Supervisions were shorter than had been anticipated, and than doctors themselves stated to be desirable. Problems concerning lack of continuity and some confusions concerning the supervision of restricted patients were apparent.

Nevertheless recidivism and relapse rates were relatively low when these patients' postdischarge careers were compared with those of other similar patients.

In the next chapter attention will be paid to individual characteristics of patients which were found to be associated with success in the community.

4 Patients' characteristics associated with reintegration

Introduction

Chapter Three described patient characteristics, their lengths of stay in hospital and their postdischarge environments. At the end of the chapter, incidents of relapse and recidivism were described. The way in which these were used to allocate 'incident' scores to patients was described briefly in Chapter Two (and more fully in Appendix One) and the results for active patients were shown in Table 2.1.

The present chapter describes some associations between patients' characteristics (and their lengths of stay in hospital) and incident scores or, in some instances, aspects of integration measured by the repertory grid score described in Chapter Two and in more detail in Appendix One.

The decision to deal with some factors as patient characteristics, rather than as environmental factors, was made on the following basis. Characteristics include aspects of a patient's individual makeup which are not subject to change by any effort on his part or by anyone else, such as his age or ethnicity; those which he acquired prior to discharge and the effects of which are for practical purposes irrevocable, such as his preadmission history, admission offence and diagnosis, length of stay in hospital and Restriction Order; and those aspects of postdischarge careers which are usually perceived to be the result of a patient's own choice, such as his marital status, involvement in alcohol abuse or refusal of medication. Environmental factors, see Chapter Five, include the role of the family and supervision, where decisions and influences of external agencies impinge more forcibly on a patient's career.

The allocation of factors to either chapter is somewhat arbitrary since, for example, it was argued on pages 24 to 26 that an acquired characteristic such as diagnosis is largely determined by social factors; and postdischarge employment, accommodation and disclosure of Special Hospital background, which are considered in Chapter Five, are matters over which patients progressively had more control, see for example, page 28. However, this chapter reviews characteristics which supervisors and patients might have in mind when assessing any individual patient's progress or when choices and decisions need to be made. Assessment and decisions can be weighed in the light of information about the careers of many similar patients.

Characteristics were selected for analysis either because they had proved of interest in previously published studies or because they were identified as being of particular interest by 'soft data' analysis of interview material and case histories. Data were not 'dredged' for all possible relationships, although the number of significant relationships found was certainly in excess of the five per cent which might have occurred by chance had that procedure been adopted. Data were collapsed into two, or occasionally three, categories whenever possible, in order to simplify analysis and presentation. Where there was no obvious 'cut off point' like that between diagnoses, categories were divised to divide patients into groups of roughly equal numbers. Some data, for example that concerning age and those scores described under 'other measures' in Appendix One, were reanalysed using other cut off points in case the arbitrary division was causing any distortion. None which would affect the interpretation of results reported here was found.

For the sake of consistency and simplicity relationships are reported throughout this book in terms of statistical significance using chi squared tests corrected for continuity when expected figures in any cell were less than ten; or occasionally Fisher's Exact Test when expected figures in any cell were less than five. Phi (or Cramer's V when appropriate) then shows the comparative strength of the association in a form which is, unlike chi, independent of the numbers involved in calculations. The relative strengths of associations of factors in an analysis can be established by introducing them in turn or in sequence. As a rough guide, probabilities greater than .05 ($p < .05$) demonstrate that relationships are most unlikely to be the result of chance; and associations of .24 or more indicate that factors are strongly linked and the relative importance of factors can be roughly assessed from this information. More sophisticated calculation attempting to establish the hierarchical importance of interrelated factors is now in hand but will take some time to complete; other tests of significance which methodologists may think more appropriate have not so far disclosed findings of more interest than those reported here.

Preadmission history

Bowden (1981) concluded after reviewing the literature that preadmission history was the most reliable predictor of postdischarge career and it was examined first. A comparison of preadmission histories with postdischarge careers confirmed the impressions already reported, that patients' postdischarge careers were less deviant than their preadmission histories.

The distribution of preadmission histories of the 330 active patients in Table 4.1 did not differ significantly from that shown for 477 patients in Table 3.1. Preadmission history therefore seems not to affect postdischarge progress from inactivity in hospital to active participation in the community.

Looking only at the totals shown in Table 4.1 it can be seen that although 59 per cent (38 per cent plus 21 per cent) of active patients had a preadmission history of inpatient hospital treatment only 37 per cent were involved in any psychiatric incident after discharge. Only 22 per cent were involved in any serious psychiatric incident (see Table 4.2 overleaf) and these included some suicide attempts which did not need hospital inpatient treatment. Similarly, although 67 per cent (38 per cent plus 29 per cent) of patients had had preadmission court appearances, only 27 per cent were involved in any criminal incident after discharge (see Table 4.1) and only 16 per cent in any serious criminal incident (see Table 4.2). Although only 12 per cent of patients when admitted had no history of court appearances or hospital admissions, about half had none after discharge (see Table 4.1).

Table 4.1
Preadmission and postdischarge incidents, %s of 330 active patients

Preadmission history   Postdischarge incidents

	Psychiatric		Criminal		All		Pread
	None	Any	None	Any	None	Any	Total
Court appearances and hospital admissions	55%	45%	69%	31%	42%	58%	[38%]
Court appearances only	67%	33%	65%	35%	42%	58%	[29%]
Hospital admissions only	60%	40%	84%	16%	56%	44%	[21%]
None known	84%	16%	84%	16%	76	24%	[12%]
Postdischarge total	63%	37%	73%	27%	49%	51%	100%

49

The full set of six tables, from three of which these percentages are extracted, can be found in Appendix Two. The significance and strength of associations which appear at the foot of all six tables, each of which includes the four types of preadmission history and one type of incident score are summarised below and a similar system of briefly summarising levels of significance and of strengths of association will be adopted throughout. In every instance the three categories for frequency are none, one, two or more. For incidents weighted for seriousness, the three categories are for scores of none, one or two, three or more except in the case of weighting for total incidents. Here the scores are none, one to three, and four or more. This increase of one point avoids distortion in the direction of seriousness which otherwise occurs when scores for nine per cent of patients with less serious incidents from both criminal and psychiatric categories were combined. Distortion in the opposite direction is negligible because less than one per cent of combined scores which totalled three included a serious incident.

Table 4.2
Preadmission and postdischarge serious (S) and less serious (LS) incidents, percentages* of 330 active patients

Preadmission history   Postdischarge incidents

	Psychiatric		Criminal		All		Pread
	LS	S	LS	S	LS	S	Total
Court appearances and hospital admissions	18%	28%	15%	16%	21%	37%	[38%]
Court appearances only	10%	23%	10%	25%	17%	42%	[29%]
Hospital admissions only	21%	19%	10%	6%	29%	16%	[21%]
None known	8%	8%	5%	11%	8	16%	[12%]
Postdischarge total	15%	22%	12%	16%	21%	30%	100%

* Rounding of percentages occasionally leads to discrepancies of one per cent between Tables 4.1 and 4.2.

Significant relationships and associations between the four types of preadmission history and postdischarge incidents can be summarised as follows:

Six tables in Appendix Two	x^2	df	sig.level	phi C.V
(i) Psychiatric incidents (frequency)	12.51	6	<.05	.13
(ii) Psychiatric incidents (weighted)	15.12	6	<.01	.15
(iii) Criminal incidents (frequency)	15.46	6	<.01	.15
(iv) Criminal incidents (weighted)	18.03	6	<.006	.17
(v) All incidents (frequency)	18.02	6	<.006	.17
(vi) All incidents (weighted)	27.64	6	<.001	.20

It is evident that there is a strong association between preadmission history and subsequent events but it was argued on page 3 that psychologically well adjusted patients may revert to their preadmission deviant lifestyle. The only fairly certain prediction which could be made from a detailed examination of the tables summarised above was that most patients with no previous record would lead a blameless and healthy life but 24 per cent would not. Of those with a previous history of both psychiatric and criminal events 58 per cent would be involved in another event but 42 per cent would be incident free.

However, preadmission history was the most influential factor in the formulation of diagnosis, perhaps because of the difficulty of making clinical observations or psychological tests, see page 24 in Chapter Three. The effect of this aspect of medical intervention in a patient's career was to assign to him a characteristic which had considerable consequences after discharge.

Admission diagnosis and postdischarge careers

At the time of discharge all the consequences of a diagnosis made years earlier may not have been foreseen by Special Hospital doctors, especially as about half of patients with either of the two major diagnoses were 'symptom free' at departure. Doctors did know that some NHS hospitals were unwilling to accept any patient who had been diagnosed as psychopathic, a fact confirmed during interviews with NHS doctors, and they were aware that this led to direct discharge into the community of many psychopaths. Evidence (see Table 3.7) of the strong association between placement of patients, of whom about half were symptom free, and admission diagnosis suggests that the latter continued to influence events, regardless of the patient's health or behaviour, after discharge.

When the set of six tables showing the distribution of psychopaths and schizophrenics for each kind of incident score, see (i) to (vi) opposite, was examined, it was found that psychopaths were more likely to reoffend and schizophrenics to relapse. Tables 4.3 and 4.4 overleaf show details of the significant though rather weak associations between these two major diagnoses and frequency of criminal and psychiatric incidents, see (i) and (iii) opposite.

There was also a significant association between diagnosis and weighted psychiatric (but not weighted criminal) incidents, schizophrenics being more likely to have serious relapses. It is arguable that only weighted incidents represent the aspects of behaviour which treatment might affect, less serious behaviour merely reflecting preadmission life style. The lack of any significant association for total incidents merely reflects the fact that the associations for criminal and psychiatric incidents are in opposite directions, and when summed these associations are concealed.

Table 4.3
Admission diagnosis by psychiatric incidents (N 288)

	None	One	Two +
Psychopathic	81 (72%)	22 (20%)	9 (8%)
Schizophrenic	98 (56%)	46 (26%)	32 (18%)

x^2= 9.22,df 2, p<.01;Cramer's V .18

Table 4.4
Admission diagnosis by criminal incidents (N 288)

	None	One	Two +
Psychopathic	72 (64%)	19 (17%)	21 (19%)
Schizophrenic	133 (76%)	28 (16%)	15 (9%)

x^2= 7.00,df 2, p<.03;Cramer's V .16

Diagnosis, supervision and deviant behaviour

It is probable that the interpretation of postdischarge incidents as criminal thus leading to court appearance, rather than symptomatic of illness thus leading to hospital admission, was partly a consequence of the type of supervisor appointed. However, diagnosis was strongly associated with allocation of either a probation officer or a social worker as supervisor, despite the high proportion of symptom free patients, see Table 4.5. Hospital social workers are shown separately to demonstrate that this finding was not merely an artefact of the supervision by hospital social workers of schizophrenics discharged from NHS hospitals; in fact NHS doctors expressed a preference for probation officers as colleagues.

Table 4.5
Main agency supervising by admission diagnosis (N 247)

	Psychopathic	Schizophrenic
Probation Service	87 (68%)	41 (32%)
Hospital social worker	8 (14%)	50 (86%)
LA social worker	15 (25%)	46 (75%)

x^2=60.47, df 2, p<.001; Cramer's V .49

Psychopaths were more likely to be supervised by probation officers, schizophrenics by social workers. Doctors and social supervisors often said that they thought this was appropriate, and social supervisors were more likely to say that they did not understand their role when they were supervising psychopaths and that they had more problems with these clients, see Table 4.6.

Table 4.6
Patient causes more problems for social supervisor by diagnosis
(N 206)

More problems?	Psychopathic	Schizophrenic
Yes	32 [38%]	29 [24%]
No	52 [62%]	93 [76%]

X^2=4.9, df 1, p<.05; phi .15

Doctors were also more likely to regard psychopaths as neither ill nor requiring treatment and were very much more likely to be seeing schizophrenics than psychopaths whom they supervised, see Tables 4.7 and 4.8 which include only patients with either of the two major diagnoses who were supervised by a psychiatrist.

Table 4.7
Patient contact with current or latest psychiatrist by diagnosis
(N 110)

Sees psychiatrist	Psychopathic	Schizophrenic
Never, rarely	25 (74%)	9 (26%)
1 to 4 times a year	22 (47%)	25 (53%)
5 or more times a year	1 (3%)	28 (97%)

X^2=31.6, df 2, p<.001; Cramer's V .53

Table 4.8
When patient last saw current psychiatrist (excluding any whose supervision had ended) by diagnosis (N 106)

Last seen	Psychopathic	Schizophrenic
Never seen or over a year ago	21 [81%]	5 [19%]
Within the last year	23 [29%]	57 [71%]

X^2=19.78, df 1, p<.001; phi .43

Neither type of supervisor was likely to attribute any deviant behaviour of a psychopath to the mental illness or disorder which had justified his detention in the Special Hospital. Supervisors of a schizophrenic might well support a defence that his behaviour resulted from illness, but in fact there was no difference in the proportions of charges which resulted from police contacts, if only those contacts are included which were made in the normal course of duty and not in connection with recalls or readmissions. Table 4.9 shows that psychopaths were significantly more likely to be contacted in this way. If contacts in connection with recalls and readmissions were to be included, contacts with schizophrenics would be more numerous but psychopaths would then be seen to be charged significantly more often as a result. Whichever set of figures is examined, police contacts with schizophrenics were of a different order to those with psychopaths.

Table 4.9
Police contact by diagnosis (N 227)

Contact	Psychopathic	Schizophrenic
Ever	68 [69%]	61 [47%]
Never	30 [31%]	68 [53%]

$$X^2=11.09, \text{ df } 1, \text{ p}<.001; \text{ phi } .22$$

It was interesting, considering psychopaths' lesser contact with psychiatrists, to find a significant association between the diagnosis of psychopathy and one of the positive aspects of integration, the aspiration not to break rules. 76 per cent of psychopaths but only 56 per cent of schizophrenics had this aspiration (p<.008; phi .24) and there was a marked association ($X^2=3.55$, 3.84 required for significance at the p<.05 level) between such an aspiration and less frequent involvement in all incidents, suggesting that involvement in deviant behaviour matched aspirations.

In view of the fact that less serious deviant behaviour of patients is probably interpreted as criminal or symptomatic of illness according to diagnosis, the most serious postdischarge offences committed by patients who reoffended were examined, to see if there were differences between patients with either of the main diagnoses. Table 4.10 shows the most serious offence which any reoffending 'active' psychopath or schizophrenic committed.

Table 4.10
Most serious postdischarge offence by diagnosis (N 91)

Offence	Psychopathic	Schizophrenic
Homicide and attempted homicide	3 (75%)	1 (25%)
Sexual	10 (71%)	4 (29%)
Arson	4 (67%)	2 (33%)
Assault	7 (33%)	14 (67%)
Acquisitive	17 (61%)	11 (39%)
Other	7 (39%)	11 (61%)

The figures for some offences in Table 4.10 (which includes eight patients with parking offences who were excluded from Tables 4.3 and 4.4) are too small to permit useful assessment of the probability of chance occurrence, but psychopaths were more likely to commit sexual offences and arson and schizophrenics were more likely to be assaultive. A higher percentage of psychopaths committed serious crimes but the data show no significant relationship between serious, less serious and no crimes for the total numbers of schizophrenics and psychopaths in the community, nor was there any significant relationship between diagnosis and weighted criminal incident scores, see page 51.

Caution is required in interpreting trends in the small number of postdischarge events, but it is remarkable that three quarters of preadmission offences of homicide or attempted homicide were by schizophrenics and that the situation appears to be reversed after discharge. The fact that schizophrenics tended to be older than psychopaths may have affected the force and frequency with which any assaults were made but it seems more likely that assaults made by schizophrenics were less likely to be regarded as intentionally homicidal. Assaults were in fact the typical schizophrenic offence both before and after treatment in the Special Hospital, see Table 3.9 and Table 4.10. The relationship between admission offence and postdischarge events is examined later, see page 61.

Diagnosis and drinking problems

Psychopaths were however more likely to have a drinking problem, see Table 4.11, and problem drinkers will be discussed in more detail later in this chapter.

Table 4.11
Patient has drinking problem by diagnosis (N 244)

Problem?	Psychopathic	Schizophrenic
Yes	32 [32%]	26 [18%]
No	68 [68%]	118 [82%]

$$x^2=6.33, \text{ df1, } p<.025; \text{ phi.16}$$

Diagnosis and rehabilitation

Psychopaths also had less occupational training after discharge, see Tables 4.12 and 4.13 and were less likely to have had sheltered employment, see Table 4.14. The figures are given as evidence of differential treatment of the two groups; the usefulness of occupational training was questioned in Chapter Three. Patients with all diagnoses expressed a wish for rehabilitation which would probably be met by appropriate social skills training. It might have been argued that the different nature of their illness made only schizophrenics suitable candidates for sheltered employment if it were not for the fact that some psychopaths were apparently accepted, see Table 4.14.

Table 4.12
Rehabilitation or training (occupational) by diagnosis (N 235)

	Psychopathic	Schizophrenic
None	76 [82%]	79 [56%]
Government training centres	12 [13%]	27 [19%]
Hospital	5 [5%]	36 [25%]

x^2=19.92, df 2, p<.001; Cramer's V .29

Table 4.13
Social skills training by diagnosis (N 236)

	Psychopathic	Schizophrenic
Training	12 [12%]	34 [24%]
None	84 [88%]	106 [76%]

x^2=5.04, df 1, p<.01; phi .15

Table 4.14
Ever in sheltered employment by diagnosis (N 243)

	Psychopathic	Schizophrenic
Yes	6 [6%]	34 [24%]
No	95 [94%]	108 [76%]

x^2=12.63, df 1, p<.001; phi .23

Diagnosis and employment

Psychopaths also had a better work record. Both schizophrenics and psychopaths had interruptions to their lives in the community; although rather more than half of all schizophrenics were readmitted to hospital and rather more than a third of psychopaths went to prison, the latter stayed in prison for longer periods than schizophrenics stayed in hospital and many schizophrenics were able to work whilst inpatients. Nevertheless, psychopaths had fewer long periods of unemployment, see Table 4.15. (All tables include only patients for whom full information was available).

Psychopaths were more likely to change jobs, see Table 4.16. It was explained in Chapter Three that patients changed jobs in order to improve their situation, changes often being a sign of initiative rather than of instability.

Table 4.15
Longest period of unemployment; and between discharge and finding first job by diagnosis (N 175;136)

| | Of unemployment | | To find first job | |
	Psych.	Schiz.	Psych.	Schiz.
Less than 6 months	41 (58%)	30 (42%)	64 (60%)	42 (40%)
6 - < 12 months	12 (38%)	20 (62%)	7 (44%)	9 (56%)
12 months or more	21 (29%)	51 (71%)	2 (14%)	12 (86%)

X^2=12.33, df2, p<.005; C's V .27: X^2=11.29, df2, p<.005; C's V .29

Table 4.16
Number of jobs by diagnosis (N 257)

	Psychopathic	Schizophrenic
Four or more	15 (71%)	6 (29%)
Two or three	37 (53%)	33 (47%)
One	38 (45%)	47 (55%)
None	14 (17%)	67 (83%)

X^2=31.52, df 3, p<.001; Cramer's V .35

The evidence that psychopaths stayed longer in their first job and were more likely to have a long period with one employer, see Table 4.17, shows that they were generally more stable in work than schizophrenics.

Table 4.17
Length of time in first job; longest time in one job by diagnosis (N160;160)

| | In first job | | Longest in one job | |
	Psych.	Schiz.	Psych.	Schiz.
Less than 6 months	30 (40%)	45 (60%)	18 (36%)	32 (64%)
6 - < 12 months	21 (57%)	16 (43%)	16 (47%)	18 (53%)
12 months or more	33 (69%)	15 (31%)	47 (62%)	29 (38%)

X^2=10.05, df2, p<.01; C's V .25: X^2=8.28, df2, p<.025; C's V .23

Despite their lack of rehabilitation, psychopaths had better work records than schizophrenics and the next two sections show that, perhaps because they entered the community more quickly, psychopaths also had more social contacts and more independently obtained accommodation than schizophrenics.

Diagnosis and relationships

Psychopaths were more successful in establishing social relationships than schizophrenics, although the associations in all tabulations for social contacts with friends, acquaintances, relatives, engaging in club or group activities, etc. are rather weak. Age, discussed briefly below, was a more important factor here than in most other associations. Proportionately more psychopaths were married than schizophrenics, see Table 4.18, and two-thirds of their marriages took place after discharge compared to two-fifths of schizophrenics'.

Table 4.18
Patients' postdischarge marital status by diagnosis (N 270)

Status	Psychopathic	Schizophrenic
Married, cohabiting	37 [35%]	37 [23%]
Separated, divorced, widowed	17 [16%]	46 [28%]
Single	53 [50%]	80 [49%]

x^2=7.54, df 2, p<.025; Cramer's V.17.

Psychopaths were less likely to be engaged in solitary leisure activities than schizophrenics and more likely to be engaged in group activities, see Table 4.19.

Table 4.19
Patients' solitary/group leisure activities by diagnosis (N 187/193)

| | Solitary | | Group | |
	Psych.	Schiz.	Psych.	Schiz.
Takes part in	40 (37%)	68 (63%)	34 (54%)	29 (46%)
Does not	44 (56%)	35 (44%)	48 (37%)	82 (63%)

x^2=6.05, df 1, p<.025; phi .19: x^2=5.05, df 1, p<.025; phi .16

Diagnosis and accommodation

Psychopaths were more likely to obtain their latest accommodation themselves but schizophrenics were more likely to receive welfare agency and hospital assistance, see Table 4.20. The usual mode of entry to the community for psychopaths, directly from the Special Hospital, accounts for the high percentage of accommodation found for them by the discharging hospital at this stage.

Psychopaths were more likely to show initiative in changing accommodation, see Table 4.21 opposite and changes were, see page 28, as in employment, usually for the better. They were less likely to remain long in hostels, see Table 4.22 opposite.

Table 4.20
How patient got first/latest accommodation by diagnosis (N 255/143)

| | First accommodation | | Latest accommodation | |
	Psych.	Schiz.	Psych.	Schiz.
Self	2 (14%)	12 (86%)	30 (58%)	22 (42%)
Wife, family, friends	48 (40%)	73 (60%)	21 (46%)	25 (54%)
Social supervisor	9 (28%)	23 (72%)	12 (35%)	22 (65%)
Hospital	42 (48%)	46 (52%)	2 (18%)	9 (82%)

X^2=7.94, df 3, p<.05; C's V .18 : X^2=7.86, df 3, p<.05; C's V .23

Table 4.21
Number of changes of accommodation by diagnosis (N 251)

	Psychopathic	Schizophrenic
Four or more	13 (62%)	8 (38%)
One to three	59 (43%)	79 (57%)
None	30 (32%)	62 (67%)

X^2=6.49, df 2, p<.05; Cramer's V .16

Table 4.22
How long in hostel by diagnosis (N 115)

	Psychopathic	Schizophrenic
Less than 6 months	22 (58%)	16 (42%)
6 < 12 months	14 (48%)	15 (52%)
1 year or more	12 (25%)	36 (75%)

X^2=10.12, df 2, p<.01; Cramer's V .30

Diagnosis: summary

Some of the associations with diagnosis discussed in this section could be attributed at least in part to symptoms of the illness diagnosed on admission. Chronic schizophrenics, for example, are likely to show less initiative and to be withdrawn. However, such patients were more likely to have remained inactive and in that event would not figure in this analysis. Moreover, more than half of the active patients were regarded as symptom free at the time of discharge. Any lack of initiative due to institutionalisation should have been equally distributed. The weight of the evidence supports the argument that diagnosis itself has influential postdischarge consequences, particularly for psychopaths, and the implications of this for patients and supervisors are discussed in Chapter Seven.

Age

The associations with diagnosis reported in the previous section could almost all be repeated showing significant but rather weaker associations with age at admission, since age was a factor associated with admission diagnosis, see Table 3.10, psychopaths being predominantly younger.

In a few predictable instances age was a stronger factor than diagnosis. Those under 30 years of age at admission were more likely be married when interviewed (Cramer's V .37 compared to .17 for the association with diagnosis in Table 4.18) and 75 per cent of their marriages took place after discharge. Age was slightly more strongly associated with involvement in criminal and weighted criminal incidents, see the summary below, than were diagnosis or preadmission history (see pages 50 to 52), in keeping with general findings in criminal statistics that there is decreasing involvement in almost all kinds of crime with advancing age; however, the association of age with other types of incidents was generally weak and attributable to the strong association between age and diagnosis (Table 3.10).

Significant relationships and associations between admission ages (dichotomised at 30 or less, 31 or more) and postdischarge incidents can be summarised as follows:

Age by:	x^2	df	sig.level	phi C.V
(i) Psychiatric incidents (frequency)	not significant			.02
(ii) Psychiatric incidents (weighted)	7.28	2	<.03	.15
(iii) Criminal incidents (frequency)	17.03	2	<.001	.23
(iv) Criminal incidents (weighted)	15.64	2	<.001	.22
(v) All incidents (frequency)	not significant			.04
(vi) All incidents (weighted)	11.01	2	<.004	.18

When examining postdischarge events, however, age at discharge was generally used in preference to age at admission, since the former more accurately represents the true association of present age with behaviour. A summary of incidents using the same dichotomy at age 30 but using age at discharge gave predictably weaker associations. Dichotomising at age 40 gave results similar to those shown above.

Various trials dichotomising or trichotomising at different ages often produced unequal distributions with some rather small numbers in some cells, but one or two interesting findings emerged where this was not the case. 61 per cent of those aged under 40 when discharged, and who completed repertory grids, saw themselves as rulebreaking compared to 43 per cent of older patients (the finding was significant at p<.04). Trichotomising at age 40 and under, 41 to 50, 51 and over showed a U-curve in self esteem, with 60 per cent of the middle age group having decreased esteem, compared to 40 per cent of the others; and fewer of this middle group thought they were less rulebreaking than when they left the Special Hospital (findings significant at p<.03 and Cramer's V .23 and .22). This group may suffer more than usual stress after discharge, since it contains a rather larger proportion of men who had spent very long periods in Broadmoor. They would have been relatively young when admitted and left as middle aged men. Low self esteem is a predictor of deviant behaviour (Kaplan, 1976) and this group may need considerable support if they are to avoid relapse and recidivism.

Younger patients were less likely to be admitted to an NHS hospital, and if admitted they were less likely to be retained long, again reflecting the association of age with diagnosis. They were, however, more likely to have parents alive and petitioning for their return to the community (parents were responsible for 43 of 51 petitions known to have been made on behalf of patients whilst they were still in the Special Hospital).

Age was also associated with admission offence (see Table 3.4) which was another component in diagnosis (see Table 3.9) and one which affected lengths of stay in hospital. The way in which admission offences were associated with postdischarge careers will be examined next, since this was the remaining influential factor associated with diagnosis and age.

Admission offence

Admission offence was more strongly associated with diagnosis (see Table 3.9) than with postdischarge incidents when all three categories of incident were cross tabulated with seven kinds of offence; the effect of diagnosis upon the perception of behaviour as criminal or symptomatic of illness cannot be discounted. The relative likelihood of various kinds of offenders being involved in any further offence or relapse is shown in Table 4.23 overleaf, where only two categories of frequency are used (none, any) to simplify presentation. The distribution is then only significant for psychiatric incidents.

Table 4.23 shows that patients whose admission offence was homicide were less likely to relapse or reoffend than any other type of offender, despite their greater likelihood of being schizophrenic, see Table 3.9 and the association between this diagnosis and relapse. 60 per cent of this group had self percepts as not rulebreaking compared to 45 per cent of all other patients. Acquisitive offenders (those whose offences were theft, burglary, larceny, fraud, etc.)

were most likely to relapse; those most prone to reoffend were patients with admission offences of assault, but further interpretations of this finding are made in the section below concerning problem drinkers.

Table 4.23
Admission offence by post discharge incidents,
active patients (N330)

Offence	Psychiatric		Criminal		All	
	None	Any	None	Any	None	Any
Homicide	50 (76%)	16 (24%)	56 (85%)	10 (15%)	41 (62%)	25 (38%)
Attempted homicide	19 (66%)	10 (34%)	21 (72%)	8 (28%)	16 (55%)	13 (45%)
Sexual	24 (73%)	9 (27%)	21 (64%)	12 (36%)	15 (46%)	18 (54%)
Arson	25 (63%)	15 (37%)	29 (73%)	11 (27%)	19 (48%)	21 (52%)
Assault	62 (58%)	45 (42%)	69 (45%)	38 (55%)	46 (43%)	61 (57%)
Acquis.	11 (39%)	17 (61%)	22 (79%)	6 (21%)	10 (36%)	18 (64%)
Other	16 (59%)	11 (41%)	22 (82%)	5 (18%)	14 (52%)	13 (48%)

x^2 (all df 6): 14.069, p<.05 : 11.46, not sig. : 8.80, not sig.

More interesting is the relationship between preadmission and postdischarge offences and Table 4.24 compares these for 112 individuals, including some who were in custody or inpatients, involved in any postdischarge offences. Details of a few 'other' crimes were not known but such offences were most unlikely to have been serious.

Table 4.24
Admission offence by most serious postdischarge offence (N 112)

Most serious postdischarge offence

Admission offence	Homicide+ att. hom.	Sexual	Arson	Ass'lt	Acquis.	Other/few not known
Homicide/att. hom.	3	1	2	4	5	15
Sexual	-	9	-	1	4	1
Arson	-	2	2	1	7	1
Assault	3	2	1	12	10	9
Acquisitive	-	-	-	3	4	3
Other	-	1	1	2	1	2

Serious offences (i.e. excluding acquisitive and 'other's) formed 85 per cent of all admission offences, see Table 3.3, and 84 per cent of these 112 patients' admission offences. For these reoffenders 45 per cent of their 'most serious postdischarge offences' were also serious. Three of the thirty with an admission offence of homicide who reoffended in some way committed a similar offence, but two were still in custody at the time. Sexual offenders who reoffended were most likely to commit a similar offence, and two of them did so whilst inpatients. The tendency therefore was for postdischarge offences to be less serious than admission offences (and of course the majority of patients did not reoffend) and some of the crimes categorised as serious were technical and not necessarily dangerous offences.

Restriction Orders

The two remaining factors which characterised patients before entry to the community were their length of stay in hospital and any Restriction Order, see page 6, still in force. Since interviews with supervisors had suggested that Restriction Orders would be a powerful factor affecting patient careers, restricted and unrestricted patients were compared for all possible differences. It was surprising to find little association between postdischarge events and Orders despite the time and energy expended in implementing them and the irritation and distress which was reported to result from them. The lack of association of Orders with lengths of stay in hospitals has already been discussed, see page 23.

There was no association between Restriction Orders and reoffending, court appearances, police contact, charges, imprisonment or readmission to hospital of any kind. Although only restricted patients were formally recalled to the Special Hospital there was no significant difference in the numbers of restricted or unrestricted patients readmitted to Broadmoor. It does not seem that an increase in the number of restricted patients would prevent recidivism or increase public safety. The way in which supervision is implemented might be more effective in forestalling relapse, see Chapter Five.

Although Restriction Orders usually made supervision mandatory, lengths of social supervisions did not differ for the restricted and unrestricted. Social supervisors reported no difference in problems with supervision of restricted or unrestricted clients. Restricted patients had less official assistance in obtaining first employment than the unrestricted, although by the time of interview only restricted patients had had official assistance in obtaining their last job. There was, surprisingly, no difference between disclosure scores (see next chapter and Appendix One) for the restricted compared to unrestricted patients.

Formal medical supervisions of restricted patients lasted longer than informal supervisions of the unrestricted, see Table 4.25 overleaf, but this did not necessarily indicate regular contact or knowledge of the patient's situation. Quality of care, discussed in detail in Chapter Five, was not associated with Restriction Orders.

Only two other factors of some consequence were associated with Restriction Orders. Firstly, reflecting the dislike with which these Orders were regarded by those professionally involved, a higher proportion of restricted patients had problems in registering with family doctors, and psychiatrists were significantly ($p < .025$) more likely to refuse to accept restricted patients; but only ten per cent of all patients encountered such problems.

Table 4.25
Length of time till formal medical supervision lapsed prior to absolute discharge (N 54) or till informal medical supervision lapsed (N 40)

Length of time	Formal	Informal
Less than 1 year	8 [15%]	29 [73%]
1 < 4 years	33 [61%]	8 [20%]
4 or more years	13 [24%]	3 [8%]

$$x^2 = 32.04, \text{ df } 2, \text{ } p < .001$$

Secondly, Restriction Orders were positively associated with cooperation in accepting medication, see Table 4.26, although interpretation of this finding should be deferred until medication is discussed later in this chapter.

Table 4.26
Restricted by refusal of medication (N 143)

	Refuses	Does not
Subject to restrictions	42 (36%)	76 (64%)
Not subject to restrictions	15 (60%)	10 (40%)

$$x^2 = 4.16, \text{ df } 1, \text{ } p < .04; \text{ phi } .19$$

Restrictions did not prevent problems at point of discharge or transfer which are described more fully in Chapter Five or cope with the major factor associated with criminal recidivism, problem drinking, discussed on page 72.

However, it was difficult to find any concrete evidence that Orders created problems for patients other than those resulting from the antipathy with which restrictions were regarded by professionals involved in supervision of patients. There was, for example, no evidence that police contacted restricted patients more frequently than unrestricted patients although they were notified of the addresses of the former. Patients were reported to regard the Order as stigmatic and for this reason, and as a constant reminder of an unhappy past, an Order may cause distress. Nevertheless, although stigma was mentioned as a problem by patients, Restriction Orders were mentioned by relatively few patients but by many doctors and social supervisors. The resentment about Orders felt by patients may in part reflect the feelings of their supervisors. Restrictions do impose burdens upon social and medical supervisors to ensure continuity of care, and upon hospital doctors to assume responsibility for aftercare of patients who have left their hospital. Such responsibilities should perhaps be incorporated into normal good practice. The effects of failures of liaison for patients, discussed in the next chapter, suggest that if statutory requirements were discontinued the rates of relapse (though not of reoffending) might increase.

Lengths of stay in hospitals

Stays in the Special Hospital

There was no evidence that longer stays in the Special Hospital (usually Broadmoor, but 34 patients had also stayed in other Special Hospitals, the majority in Park Lane) were associated with better outcomes for patients, rather the reverse. For all 588 patients there was no significant association between any outcome measure and length of stay, except that patients with very long stays were more likely to remain 'inactive'. However, the association was weak (phi .14) and vanished for those under 40 when the relationship was 'controlled' for age. ('Controlling' means that the tables were extended to introduce a new variable, age in this case, redistributing the data so that the effect of this introduction could be examined. To avoid overloading the text with tables these are not always presented when descriptions of the findings seem adequate, as in this instance. However, Tables 4.27 and 4.28 demonstrate the procedure, including a new variable, diagnosis, in tabulations which had previously shown only lengths of stay in hospital by incidents). Failure of patients to move to the 'active' sample was therefore attributable to age at discharge rather than to length of stay in the Special Hospital. For all active patients there were no significant differences related to lengths of stay, contrary to findings by Black (1982) whose patients, however, had different characteristics which are discussed in Chapter Six.

Differences were found between schizophrenics and psychopaths when the repertory grid measure and incident scores were examined. 72 per cent of 73 schizophrenics who stayed in the Special Hospital for six or more years saw themselves as 'more rulebreaking at interview than when they left the Special Hospital' compared with 54 per cent of those who left earlier. This was not merely an indicator of reaction against institutionalisation since only 57 per cent of 23 psychopaths who stayed in the Special Hospital for six years or more had a similar self percept. (Lengths of stay like those shown in Table 4.27 were used and the finding was significant at p<.05, Cramer's V .28).

It is possible that these may have been patients who were refusing medication after discharge, bearing in mind that those prescribed medication were mainly schizophrenics. There was no association between this self percept and known or almost certain cessation of medication, discussed later in this chapter.

The relationship between postdischarge refusal of medication and length of stay might seem remote. However, there were some patients known to have refused medication in the Special Hospital until they appreciated that the particular consultant who was responsible for their discharge would not recommend it until they accepted medication. These were patients most likely to refuse medication after discharge; and there would have to be many more than those known to have ceased medication if cessation did account for the significant number of self percepts of more rulebreaking after discharge amongst the long stay schizophrenics. The practice of consultants varied and some would not discharge patients who were on medication.

Other grid findings were not statistically significant but 11 per cent more patients leaving after three but in less than six years had lower grid scores for integration (using the score best matched with doctors' assessments, see Table 2.4, since these findings were of most interest to doctors) than others. This was partly attributable to falling self esteem (68 per cent of those leaving in less than three years had increased self esteem, compared to 57 per cent of those staying longer); and partly attributable to the decline in aspirations to be independent, from 95 per cent of those leaving in under three years to 87 per cent of those staying six years or more. All these grid findings show poorer outcomes for longer stays in the Special Hospital.

Although there was no association for all patients between postdischarge incidents and lengths of stay in the Special Hospital, when the data were controlled for diagnosis there was an association for psychopaths, see Tables 4.27 and 4.28 opposite. All three periods are shown and again there is a return to a higher proportion of good outcomes for patients with the longest stays which disappears for those aged 40 or less when the data are controlled for age. For psychopaths, whether deviant behaviour was interpreted as symptomatic of illness or as criminal, it was less frequent in older men. In fact there is a trend, though much less marked and not statistically significant, for schizophrenic behaviour to follow a similar pattern.

How should these significant associations of length of stay with more incident scores for psychopaths but not for schizophrenics be interpreted? The lack of association between length of stay and incidents for schizophrenics may indicate either that length of stay is immaterial or that the time of discharge is well judged. Special Hospital consultants would probably prefer the latter explanation but

other possibilities should perhaps be borne in mind: a proportion of
these discharges were recommended by Mental Health Tribunals
apparently against the advice of the consultant concerned, more
patients leaving after three but in less than six years had low grid
scores for integration regardless of diagnosis, and the apparent
improvements in the very long stay figures are almost entirely
attributable to the effect of age.

Table 4.27
Length of stay in Special Hospital by postdischarge psychiatric
incidents controlled for diagnosis (N 288)

Length of stay	Psychopaths' Incidents		Schizophrenics' Incidents	
	None	Any	None	Any
Less than 3 years	18 (86%)	3 (14%)	29 (52%)	27 (48%)
3 > 6 years	26 (61%)	17 (39%)	34 (58%)	25 (42%)
6 or more years	37 (77%)	11 (23%)	35 (57%)	26 (43%)

X^2= 5.45, df 2, p<.05; Cramer's V .21 : X^2= not significant

Table 4.28
Length of stay in Special Hospital by postdischarge criminal
incidents controlled for diagnosis (N 288)

Length of stay	Psychopaths' Incidents		Schizophrenics' Incidents	
	None	Any	None	Any
Less than 3 years	16 (76%)	5 (24%)	42 (75%)	14 (25%)
3 > 6 years	21 (49%)	22 (51%)	44 (75%)	15 (25%)
6 or more years	35 (73%)	13 (27%)	47 (77%)	14 (23%)

X^2= 7.32, df 2, p<.05; Cramer's V .23 : X^2= not significant

The effects of age are concealed by using 'less than three years'
and 'three or more years' to dichotomise stays (the dichotomy adopted
by Black, 1982), see Table 4.29.

Table 4.29
Length of stay (dichotomised) in Special Hospital by postdischarge
psychiatric and criminal incidents, psychopaths only (N 112)

Length of stay	Psychiatric incidents		Criminal incidents	
	None	Any	None	Any
Less than 3 years	18 (86%)	3 (14%)	16 (76%)	5 (26%)
3 or more years	63 (69%)	28 (31%)	56 (62%)	35 (38%)

These figures (though there is now no statistically significant difference between the two periods) could be used to support the following argument. Psychopaths are not mentally ill but if they are not mad on arrival a third become so after three years: moreover, those staying longer are more prone to be involved in criminal activities after leaving, despite the general decrease in criminal activities with increasing age.

Alternatively, it could be argued that those most ill and most prone to reoffend and relapse are retained longer in the interests of public safety. However, detention for long periods can only be regarded as custodial when no improvement results from longer treatment. This argument is also weakened by the evidence that patients with admission offences of homicide are detained longer in the Special Hospital than other offenders but are less likely than others to be involved in postdischarge incidents regardless of their length of stay.

Yet another explanation may be, see page 26, that some of those diagnosed as psychopaths are embryonic mentally ill patients. This argument is supported by the evidence of a high incidence of postdischarge psychiatric admissions. The incidence is lower than that for schizophrenics, although this in turn may be due to the reluctance of NHS hospitals to admit any patients with a diagnosis of psychopathy. The greater incidence of postdischarge criminal incidents for psychopaths, it has already been argued, could also result from a combination of preadmission factors which led to the initial diagnosis which subsequently reinforced perceptions of their deviant behaviour as criminal.

Since lengths of stay varied for different kinds of offenders, outcomes for each kind of offence were examined to see if the data supported any claim that long stays did in fact change behaviour. The earlier three period categorisation was used, to avoid any possibility that beneficial effects of long stays might be concealed.

Homicides and sexual offenders were more likely to stay longer (see Table 3.3). For 112 'active' homicides there was no significant difference between the percentages of these patients involved in postdischarge incidents regardless of their length of stay, although the percentages of relapse and recidivism varied slightly in the same pattern as for all offenders. 82 per cent of those discharged in the first three years after admission did not relapse; only 67 per cent of those discharged after three but in less than six years did not; 77 per cent of those with long stays did not.

There were only 33 sexual offenders but a third of those discharged early did not reoffend; 25 per cent of those leaving after three to five years did not reoffend; and 82 per cent of those with long stays did not reoffend. Of those discharged in the first three years none relapsed; 75 per cent of those leaving after three but in less than six years and 68 per cent of those staying longer did not relapse. However, because sexual offenders and homicides had very long mean stays in hospital, see page 22, advancing age (especially for sexual offenders) influenced these results.

When all these findings were controlled for age, there were negligible differences between postdischarge reoffences or relapses for those over 30 at admission, regardless of offence or length of stay. The usual pattern for percentages of relapse and reoffence was only apparent for those aged under 30 on admission. The data were then examined for the 107 assaultive patients, whose stays were spread evenly over the whole three periods and whose ages were also evenly distributed. This is the only tabulation for a separate type of offender presented in detail, see Table 4.30.

Table 4.30

Length of stay in Special Hospital, active patients with admission offence of assault, by postdischarge psychiatric and criminal incidents (N 107)

Length of stay	Psychiatric incidents		Criminal incidents	
	None	Any	None	Any
Less than three years	18 (49%)	19 (51%)	27 (73%)	10 (27%)
3 > 6 years	24 (62%)	15 (38%)	22 (56%)	17 (44%)
Six or more years	20 (65%)	11 (35%)	20 (65%)	11 (35%)

There was no significant relationship between lengths of stay and postdischarge incidents in Table 4.30 either, although there were slightly fewer relapses amongst those leaving after three but in less than six years than amongst long stayers. However, bearing in mind the numbers involved, differences were negligible. There is faint justification here, and none supported by statistically significant evidence, for keeping schizophrenic patients (assaultive patients were predominantly schizophrenic) in the Special Hospital for more than three years. For psychopaths there was a positive and significant relationship between long stays and more involvement in both psychiatric and criminal incidents, see Tables 4.27 and 4.28.

Summarising, there is no statistically significant evidence of any improvement in patients' behaviour on grounds of length of stay of more than three years in the Special Hospital. The small reduction in criminal incidents for patients with very long stays is almost certainly a reflection of the general decline in criminal activities of older men which is bound to be a factor when stays of over five years are considered. If all patients were incarcerated until they were elderly the figures for recidivism would be improved but this is hardly a justification for retaining patients in a hospital where treatment is unavailing, even if it is thought to be an appropriate measure on grounds of law and order. All the hard evidence suggests that in general shorter stays are associated with more success; and that, although it is likely that at least some patients with longer stays are those with more difficult behaviour problems, much longer stays are no more likely to be associated with success than moderately long stays.

Stays in NHS hospitals

There was no significant association between any lengths of stay in NHS hospitals and incident measures, although there was a trend for those leaving earlier to be more often involved in criminal incidents. 29 per cent of those leaving within a year, 21 per cent of those who stayed for one or two years and 13 per cent of those who stayed for over two years being so involved. This may, however, merely reflect an association between hospitalisation and a subsequent greater likelihood that deviant events will be perceived as symptoms of illness, an argument supported by earlier findings concerning less frequent police contact with schizophrenics.

The more positive aspects of integration measured by repertory grid scores supported the conclusion that hospitals were discharging quickly patients who were most likely to become well integrated, since nine of the 13 patients who completed grids and left the transfer hospital in less than three months were high scorers on the measure of integration and also had increased self esteem, though the numbers are too small to expect statistical significance. There was a significant decrease in grid scores for integration amongst those who left the transfer hospital after two years and the strength of association was quite high (Cramer's V .26). The significant association was with the grid score which best accorded with psychiatrists' assessments (see Table 2.4). It is therefore likely that clinicians assessed all these patients as 'doing (equally) well' but the grid finding supports assertions of NHS psychiatrists that long stays led to deterioration of some unspecified kind in patients who were clinically fit to leave. Amongst those who completed grids and who stayed longer in the transfer hospitals there were higher percentages of people with lowered self esteem, lower aspirations and poorer self percepts, with strengths of association varying from Cramer's V .21 to .23. It is also interesting to note that the majority of these patients were schizophrenics, for whom no such associations were found with lengths of stay in the Special Hospital. Poor integration may be the result of frustration, also mentioned by psychiatrists, felt by Special Hospital patients when other patients with more obvious symptoms of illness left after short spells in the NHS hospital. This would have been an uncommon experience in the Special Hospital.

Availability of employment or differences in the kind of accommodation available were, rather surprisingly, not factors associated with early discharge. These aspects of patients' postdischarge careers are discussed again in Chapter Five.

One finding, not statistically significant, see Table 4.31, but included because the percentages may interest those concerned with Special Hospital management, was that patients who were transferred from Broadmoor to NHS hospitals tended to have longer stays than patients who had first stayed in another Special Hospital, almost always Park Lane, and were then transferred. ·

Table 4.31
Length of stay in transfer hospital by prior transfer (or not) to other Special Hospital (N 279)

	Length of stay in NHS hospital		
	> 1 year	1 > 2 years	2 + years
Direct to NHS hospital	105 (41%)	69 (27%)	82 (32%)
First to other Special Hosp.	11 (46%)	10 (42%)	3 (13%)

Did those responsible think, misguidedly, see pages 14 and 16, that total stays in two Special Hospitals must have been longer? Or was the medical history supplied by the second Special Hospital more optimistic because no one had seen the patient at an earlier stage? Or was the regime at Park Lane, at that time a small unit opened before the large permanent institution was built, a better preparation for reentry to the wider community? The figures only permit speculation but there was no apparent difference between characteristics of the two groups of patients which could account for the trend.

The lack of any other significant findings may be in part because lengths of stay in NHS hospitals are influenced to a much greater degree by factors other than patient health or public policy than are stays in the Special Hospitals. It was apparent that pressures for NHS hospital beds in some areas were much greater than in others and this alone would have influenced lengths of stay, as would the availability of social work and other staff necessary to complete the various procedures involved in discharging restricted patients and to organise accommodation if the patient lacked the initiative to do so for himself. It has also already been mentioned that staff differed in their knowledge of, and sophistication in dealing with, procedures for discharging restricted patients.

Summarising, there was no significant association between lengths of stay in NHS hospitals and any incident measures, but those discharged early from NHS hospitals tended to have high scores for integration and increased self esteem.

Of all the preceding factors thought likely to influence

71

postdischarge careers, diagnosis was the one most often associated with events; it is arguable that preadmission history, age and admission offence were often associated with postdischarge events because of interrelationships with each other and with diagnosis. However, all subsequent analyses have been examined for possible hidden effects of each of these factors (and also of ethnicity, a factor considered below). If no comment is made it may be assumed that no such relationship was found.

Problem drinking

One of the most important findings concerned those 18 per cent of all patients in the active sample known to have a drink problem. The association between problem drinking and involvement in criminal incidents was strong, see Table 4.32.

Table 4.32
Drinking problem by postdischarge incidents - active patients (N330)

	Psychiatric Incidents		Criminal Incidents		All Incidents	
Problem?	None	Any	None	Any	None	Any
Yes	29 (48%)	31 (52%)	25 (42%)	35 (58%)	13 (22%)	47 (78%)
No	178 (66%)	92 (34%)	215 (80%)	55 (20%)	148 (55%)	122 (45%)

x^2, all df 1:
6.5, p<.025, phi.14 : 35.67, p<.001, phi.33 : 21.6, p<.001, phi.26

This relatively small group of patients formed nearly two fifths of reoffenders and nearly a third of 'relapsers and offenders'. Tables 4.33 below and 4.34 opposite show that they also formed nearly half of patients committing serious or frequent offences (and they were, as a consequence, responsible for 79 per cent of serious offences committed by active patients).

Table 4.33
Drinking problem by seriousness of postdischarge criminal incidents, active patients (N330)

Criminal incidents

Problem?	None	Less serious	Serious
Yes	25 [10%]	12 [32%]	23 [44%]
No	215 [90%]	26 [68%]	29 [56%]

x^2=38.032, df 2, p<.001

Table 4.34
Drinking problem by frequency of postdischarge criminal incidents,
active patients (N330)

| | Criminal incidents | | |
Problem?	None	One	More
Yes	25 [10%]	19 [36%]	16 [43%]
No	215 [90%]	34 [64%]	21 [57%]

$$X^2=36.47, \text{ df } 2, \text{ p}<.001$$

74 per cent of these problem drinkers had had this problem at admission. Although after their stay in the Special Hospital 43 per cent did not return to drinking, 57 per cent did so and 15 patients who had no such problem at admission had one after discharge, see Table 4.35. A rather similar pattern was observed when preadmission and postdischarge drug abuse was examined, but the total numbers involved (32 preadmission and 17 after discharge) were smaller; and a slightly higher proportion (59 per cent) did not return to drug abuse after discharge but with such small numbers differences in percentages are exaggerated. The number of drug abusers was too small for any useful analysis of their involvement in postdischarge incidents.

Table 4.35
Preadmission and postdischarge drinking problems,
active patients (N281)

| | Postdischarge problem? | |
Preadmission problem?	Yes	No
Yes	43 (57%)	32 (43%)
No	15 (7%)	191 (93%)

$$X^2=81.06, \text{ df } 1, \text{ p}<.001; \text{ phi } .54$$

There were no significant associations between problem drinking and age, ethnicity or restrictions. More psychopaths than schizophrenics were problem drinkers and a higher percentage (32 per cent) of psychopaths than schizophrenics (18 per cent) were problem drinkers. The difference was significant ($p<.025$, phi .16). Rather surprisingly there were no diagnoses of depression for any problem drinker. More worrying was the fact that problem drinkers were significantly more likely ($p<.003$, Cramer's V .25) to have had admission offences of assault and attempted homicide than other patients although only five per cent of problem drinkers had admission offences of homicide. However, only two per cent of problem drinkers were admitted for 'other' relatively trivial offences and more than half therefore had a violent admission offence. Also, there was a trend for more problem drinkers (57 per cent) to be in the younger age group than in the group aged over 30 on admission (43 per cent) and younger patients were more likely to be involved in criminal activities.

Any patient with a drink problem after discharge is therefore a cause for concern. Unfortunately these patients were also likely to have characteristics such as youth, a criminal history or a diagnosis of psychopathy, which were associated with poorer quality aftercare, evidence for which will be discussed in Chapter Five.

Attitudes amongst supervisors varied from area to area. Some patients were recalled at the first sign of a drinking problem, sometimes against the wishes of the local supervisors. Others reported still to have a drinking problem remained in the community. They were often regarded as a nuisance rather than a danger especially in areas where heavy drinking was culturally acceptable, even when their behaviour was aggressive and their admission offence had been associated with heavy drinking. Doctors were sometimes proud of the fact that their hospital staff could deal with patients who became aggressive after drinking; but it seems necessary to sound a warning about patients who drink heavily.

Recidivism by patients might be reduced if time spent in the closed environment could be used to greater advantage to deal with this particular aspect of their problems. Their addiction must be psychological, since physical dependence would have been overcome during their stay in the Special Hospital, unless illicit alcohol is very freely available in Broadmoor (a number of patients did say that it could be obtained). Although staff can claim a success rate of 43 per cent who had not returned to problem drinking it is likely that in this closed institutional environment alcohol is regarded as a major pleasure to which patients expect to return. It might be appropriate for the Special Hospitals to place more stress on attitudes adopted by institutions dealing specifically with addicts.

Ethnicity

Some reference has been made in earlier chapters to the effects of ethnicity and all the findings related to this characteristic are summarised here.

Incidence

75 per cent of patients were British and their parents were born in this country. Six per cent (35) were Europeans, some of whom had been displaced persons with concentration camp or other very disturbed wartime backgrounds. Four per cent were Irish, four per cent were of other nationalities including Australians, Canadians,

North Americans and South Americans, and there were a few patients from Middle or Far Eastern countries of whom one or two might be borderline 'nonwhite'. 12 per cent were clearly nonwhite, more accurately black or brown: the term 'nonwhite' is used because it is briefer but the nonmale author apologises for any offence this negative term may cause. Most were West Indians, some were Asian Indians and a very few were Africans.

Despite some misgivings, two factors seemed to justify classification on this crude basis. Analysis of interview data disclosed two common beliefs, firstly that this group, of whichever nationality or race, reacted particularly poorly to confinement, and secondly that they were especially prone to police harrassment. Data relating to both factors were examined.

Ethnicity and diagnoses

Diagnoses were significantly distributed for all patients by the ethnic categories listed above. The British and Irish had only slightly more schizophrenic than psychopathic diagnoses; for all other patients rather more than two thirds of all diagnoses were of schizophrenia. To avoid any possible confusion due to the inclusion of white immigrants, the analysis which follows compares only data for the nonwhite group described above and data for white Britons. Using this categorisation, there was a significant difference between the 92 per cent of nonwhites and 64 per cent of white Britons amongst all patients who had diagnoses of schizophrenia, see Table 4.36 (and see page 16 for an explanation of the three 'samples').

Table 4.36
Ethnicity by major diagnoses for three 'samples' of nonwhite and white British patients

Ethnicity	Active sample (N 258)		Core sample (N 323)	
	Psych.	Schiz.	Psych.	Schiz.
Nonwhite	4 (9%)	40 (91%)	4 (8%)	44 (92%)
White Britons	98 (45%)	116 (54%)	100 (36%)	175 (64%)

X^2 =19.06, df 1, p<.001; phi .26 : X^2=13.45, df 1, p<.001, phi .19

Ethnicity	Whole sample (N 438)	
	Psych.	Schiz.
Nonwhite	5 (8%)	57 (92%)
White Britons	136 (36%)	240 (64%)

X^2=17.99, df 1, p<.001, phi .19

There were 47 nonwhites in the active sample, see Table 4.36, where the association between schizophrenic diagnosis and colour was strongest. Three had 'other' illnesses. These 47 formed 16 per cent of the group of active patients composed of nonwhites and white Britons only.

There was a slightly higher incidence of schizophrenia amongst white immigrants and it is possible that the stress of adapting to a different cultural pattern may also have affected some nonwhites. Other stresses resulting from withstanding colour prejudice may have predisposed nonwhites to manifest behaviour which attracted a diagnosis of schizophrenia. Case histories also suggested that some kinds of behaviour acceptable within the nonwhite ethnic group, for example the language of Rastafarians, may have been interpreted by doctors as symptomatic of schizophrenic illness.

If diagnoses which resulted from misinterpretation of cultural differences accounted for some diagnoses of schizophrenia for the nonwhite group, at least some of the greater 'activity' amongst nonwhite schizophrenics reported below might be because they had been misdiagnosed.

Ethnicity and stays in the Special Hospital

It was found that nonwhites were significantly more ($p<.01$) likely to have shorter stays in Broadmoor, only two nonwhites having spent more than ten years there. However, this finding most probably reflected the smaller proportion of nonwhites in the United Kingdom in earlier decades. Proportionately fewer nonwhites would have been admitted. The differences in postdischarge careers between the two groups are more interesting.

Ethnicity and stays in transfer hospitals

There was no significant difference between mean lengths of stay in the NHS hospitals to which patients were transferred after leaving the Special Hospital for nonwhites or whites, or for these two groups when controlled for age or diagnosis, and the difference in lengths of stay in the Special Hospital is almost certainly an artefact of changing population patterns in the country. However, if respondents to interviews were correct in thinking that nonwhite patients reacted particularly badly to institutional life, it might be expected that they would be discharged earlier than white Britons.

The unexpected lack of difference in mean lengths of stays in hospital was not explained by nonwhites' admission offences (graver admission offences were associated with long stays in Special and other hospitals, see page 22). Despite their overwhelming diagnoses as schizophrenic, nonwhites were half as likely to have been admitted for homicide as white Britons and less likely to have been admitted for attempted homicide, see Table 4.37. On that account alone it would be expected that they would have been discharged earlier than white Britons. The higher proportion of assaults for nonwhites is still less than might be anticipated from patients mainly diagnosed as schizophrenic, who were therefore significantly more likely to have been assaultive as well as homicidal, see Table 3.9. Regardless of their reported reaction to hospital life and the nature of their offences their stays were as long as those of white Britons.

The explanation for the unexpected similarity in mean lengths of stay may lie in the fact that almost all nonwhites were eventually discharged. The rarity with which nonwhites remained inactive is consistent with the view that their doctors thought that they reacted poorly to hospital life, although some attitudes discussed below may also account for this phenomenon.

Table 4.37
Ethnicity by admission offence, all/active white Britons and nonwhite patients (N 510/296)

Offence	All		Active	
	White Brit.	Nonwhite	White Brit.	Nonwhite
Homicide	125 [28%]	10 [14%]	54 [22%]	5 [11%]
Attempted homicide	43 [10%]	5 [7%]	24 [10%]	3 [6%]
Sexual	39 [9%]	6 [9%]	25 [10%]	5 [11%]
Arson	46 [10%]	2 [3%]	35 [14%]	2 [4%]
Assault	121 [27%]	33 [48%]	71 [29%]	25 [53%]
Acquisitive	33 [8%]	5 [7%]	21 [8%]	4 [9%]
Other	34 [8%]	8 [12%]	19 [8%]	3 [6%]

$X^2=17.63$, df 6, p<.007; C's V .19: $X^2=13.44$, df 6, p<.05; C's V .21

Nonwhite patients were, see Table 4.38, more likely to be in the active sample despite their more usual diagnosis of schizophrenia, which was associated with inactivity, see Table 4.39 overleaf.

Table 4.38
Ethnicity by activity, core sample (N 375)

Ethnicity	Inactive	Active
Nonwhite	4 [5%]	47 [16%]
White Britons	75 [95%]	249 [84%]

$X^2=5.32$, df 1, p<.02; phi .12

Almost a third of schizophrenics compared to three per cent of psychopaths were inactive, see Table 4.39. Almost all nonwhites had been diagnosed as schizophrenic on admission, see Table 4.36, but only eight per cent were 'inactive' compared to 36 per cent of all white Britons in the core sample.

Table 4.39
Admission diagnosis by activity (N 365)

Diagnosis	Inactive	Active
Psychopathic	3 [4%](3%)	112 [39%](97%)
Schizophrenic	73 [96%](29%)	177 [61%](71%)

$$x^2=32.19, \text{ df } 1, \text{ } p<.001; \text{ phi } .30$$

Nonwhites discharged from hospital when white Britons with similar characteristics might have remained inactive would probably still have had relatively long stays. When included in calculations their longer stays would increase the mean length of stay for all active nonwhites.

Ethnicity and age

In addition, age was a more salient factor associated with both diagnosis and activity for nonwhites than for white Britons. Amongst younger (under 35) active patients 47 per cent of white Britons (compared to 64 per cent of their whole age range) but 90 per cent of nonwhites (compared to 92 per cent of their whole age range) were schizophrenic. There were no nonwhite inactive schizophrenics aged under 30. Amongst older active patients or the inactive of all ages there were similar proportions of schizophrenics who were white Britons or nonwhites.

Attitudes

There were therefore some common characteristics amongst young nonwhite patients (almost all diagnosed as schizophrenics) and another group of patients, those diagnosed as psychopaths. The latter patients were also more likely to be young and 'active'. Careful examination of interview data suggested that the presence of at least some of these groups of patients in the community rather than in hospital might be due to community attitudes. Doctors often referred to young nonwhite (mainly schizophrenic) and to psychopathic patients as not in need of care; and as arrogant, demanding, and generally failing to play the deferential patient role. These patients did not, however, perceive themselves as any more independent than other patients. Indeed, although there was no significant difference between nonwhite and white British patients' scores on the grid measure of integration or any aspects of integration, there was a trend for more (five per cent) nonwhite patients to perceive themselves as dependent. The demeanour of both kinds of patient may be incorrectly interpreted as suggesting more independence than they feel. The recurrence of the term 'demanding' suggests that such patients are aware of a need for support, but this probably needs to be of a specialised kind from practitioners skilled in establishing rapport with the young or nonwhite deviant. Evidence that better scores for reintegration were recorded when there was some rapport between supervisor and client or patient will be discussed in the next chapter.

Ethnicity and police harrassment

Although the number of nonwhites for whom information was available was relatively small, these 32 patients were contacted significantly more frequently than white Britons by the police, see Table 4.40, though the association is weak. Contacts refer only to calls at the patient's home or place of work, or to stops in the street or other public places which were made in the normal course of police duty. Any made when assisting with readmissions or recalls are omitted.

Table 4.40
Ethnicity by police contact (N 236)

Ethnicity	Any contact	No contact
Nonwhite	23 (72%)	9 (28%)
White Britons	107 (52%)	97 (48%)

$$X^2=3.89, \text{ df } 1, \text{ } p<.05\text{: phi } .13$$

A significantly higher proportion of nonwhites than white Britons appeared in court, see Table 4.41, which also includes only patients for whom this information was available and the association is still weak.

Table 4.41
Ethnicity by court appearances (N 258)

Ethnicity	Court appearance	No appearance
Nonwhite	15 (45%)	18 (55%)
White Britons	60 (27%)	165 (73%)

$$X^2=4.93, \text{ df } 1, \text{ } p<.05\text{; phi } .14$$

It was necessary to determine whether frequent police contact eventually provided material for a charge to be brought, perhaps of a relatively trivial nature, or whether the court appearances were evidence that more frequent contacts by the police were justified. 'Most serious offences after discharge' were examined, see Table 4.42 overleaf.

Table 4.42
Ethnicity by most serious postdischarge offence (N 106)

	Nonwhite	All others
Homicide	- [0%]	4 [5%]
Attempted homicide	1 [6%]	1 [1%]
Sexual	3 [17%]	12 [14%]
Arson	- [0%]	6 [7%]
Assault	5 [28%]	18 [20%]
Acquisitive	2 [11%]	29 [33%]
Other	7 [39%]	18 [20%]
Total	18 [101%]	88 [100%]
	(20%)	(80%)

If offences are collapsed to two categories, 'all separately listed offences' and 'others' there is a suggestive but not statistically significant association (X^2=3.2; phi .16) between the kinds of offences committed and ethnicity. Nonwhites were more likely to commit 'other', relatively trivial offences. If the usual practice adopted throughout this book is adopted, combining acquisitive with 'other', there is no difference between the two groups. Nonwhites were less likely to commit acquisitive offences, none committed arson and roughly the same percentage of nonwhites and others committed sexual and homicidal offences. Although nonwhites were slightly more likely to commit assaults than white Britons (to be expected due to the very high proportion of nonwhite schizophrenics) the most common (39 per cent) serious offence committed by nonwhites was 'other', generally of a trivial nature. It does seem that frequent police contact with nonwhites resulted more often in charges of a trivial nature.

Moreover, all the evidence concerning police contacts shows that these were more frequent for psychopathic patients (see Table 4.9) and younger patients (see Table 4.43, and Table 4.44 opposite; there were only seven contacts at work).

Table 4.43
Police contact at home by age (N 271)

	30 and under	31 and over
Any police contact	75 (74%)	27 (26%)
None	74 (44%)	95 (56%)

X^2=22.73, df 1, p<.001; phi .29

Nonwhites did not differ significantly in age from the rest of the active sample; but they were significantly more likely to be schizophrenic (see Table 4.36) so that contact should have been less frequent if they received the same treatment as white patients.

Table 4.44
Police contact generally (i.e. neither at home nor at work, most often in the street or some other public place) by age (N 263)

	30 and under	31 and over
Any police contact	46 (74%)	16 (26%)
None	102 (51%)	99 (49%)

$$x^2=10.58, \text{ df } 1, \text{ p<.005; phi .20}$$

Controlling Table 4.40 for diagnosis reduced the strength of the association for psychopaths as might be anticipated from the very small number involved, but the relationship between schizophrenic nonwhites and frequent police contact was stronger (phi .28). 76 per cent of nonwhite schizophrenics compared to 42 per cent of white schizophrenics were frequently contacted by the police. Controlling for age hardly affected the association between ethnicity and police contact except for men aged over 45 where it weakened (phi .17) in keeping with the usual trend for criminal statistics of all kinds to have lesser relevance for older men.

The weight of the evidence supports the belief that nonwhites are contacted more frequently than whites with similar characteristics and there is no evidence that this was justified. For nonwhite patients the usual perceptions which divide the 'sick' from the 'criminal' seemed to be in abeyance so far as the police were concerned. The findings here also confirm the necessity for treating figures for nonwhite recidivism with caution; more frequent contact resulted in more frequent court appearances, though the charges tended to be less serious than those brought against white Britons.

Ethnicity and relapse

When details of relapse were examined rather similar results were found. Nonwhites tended to have fewer (though not significantly fewer) psychiatric 'incidents' than white Britons, although since they were predominantly schizophrenic they should have had significantly more, see Table 4.3. There was also no significant difference between the seriousness of relapse for active nonwhites and white Britons, although schizophrenics would be expected to have more serious relapses, see page 51. The behaviour of these nonwhite patients was better than might be expected given their diagnoses and may confirm the belief that hospital is an unsuitable environment for at least some of them; but it may also give credence to the suggestion that some misdiagnoses had been made.

Ethnicity and grid measure of reintegration

The repertory grid measure of reintegration into the community showed no statistically significant differences between active nonwhites and white Britons although 64 per cent of nonwhites had high scores compared to 50 per cent of white Britons, a finding consistent with the results reported above.

Ethnicity and refusal of medication

A higher percentage of nonwhites than white Britons refused medication, see Table 4.45, and this may have contributed to supervisors' reported views about arrogant behaviour. It will be seen in the following section that there was no association between cessation of medication and relapse, rather the reverse. Nonwhites also relapsed less often than might be expected, given their diagnoses. There was also evidence, see Table 4.46, that patients (from all ethnic groups) who resented supervision had high scores for integration. If misdiagnoses for nonwhites were indeed frequent, this alone might account for much reported arrogance and resistance to treatment.

Table 4.45
Ethnicity by refusal of medication (N 153)

Refusal?	White Britons	Nonwhites
Yes	33 [28%]	16 [52%]
No	86 [72%]	18 [48%]

x^2=6.38, df 1, p<.025; phi .20

Table 4.46
Resentment of supervision by grid scores for integration (N 139)

Resented supervision?	Low score (1-4)	High score (5-7)
Yes	5 [8%]	25 [33%]
No	58 [92%]	18 [67%]

x^2=11.25, df 1, p<.001; phi .28

In summary, despite some problems revealed by supervisors' comments, less hospital treatment than other similar groups of patients, and some police harrassment, nonwhites showed a trend to behave more acceptably and to be better integrated than other patients with similar characteristics.

Cessation of medication

64 per cent of active patients diagnosed as schizophrenic on admission (and nine per cent of psychopaths) were reported to be taking major tranquillisers at the date of interview, 36 per cent were not. 80 per cent of patients taking major tranquillisers had a self percept as dependent compared to 29 per cent of those not on medication, a strong as well as significant association ($p < .001$, phi .33). Of those diagnosed as schizophrenic and not on medication, 76 per cent were incident free compared to 47 per cent of those reported to be taking medication. This would be in accord with a common sense view that those who were not prescribed medicine were more likely to be well.

Nevertheless, doctors were often uneasy about ceasing medication and some who had attempted to do so with a patient whose symptoms then returned were often reluctant to try again. It was encouraging, therefore to find no significant association between outcomes for those reported to have ceased taking medication prescribed at discharge and those still on medication, when only patients about whose medication there were no conflicting reports were included. Percentages of each group involved in each type of incident were almost identical. This would accord with the view that doctors were demonstrating nice judgement in cessation of medication. It could also be argued that medication was less effective than was generally supposed, or at least need not be continued indefinitely. Some patients had ceased medication without the approval of their doctor. There were 19 patients who had almost certainly ceased, although there was a slight element of doubt since in seven instances the doctor reported that the patient was taking medicine although he and his social supervisor denied this, and in twelve other cases cessation was assumed since no or very few appointments to receive medication had been kept over a long period of time. These patients were incident free and when they were added to those known certainly to have ceased medication, there was a significant difference favouring those who had stopped, see Table 4.47 overleaf.

The strength of the association is weak but it is in the opposite direction to that forecast by Special Hospital doctors; and it is contrary to the perceptions of those supervisors who thought that patients who constantly refused medication were more likely to relapse. The expectations of these clinical and social supervisors were based on the unrepresentative patients who were recalled or readmitted, some of whom had ceased medication either on their own initiative, or on the advice of their doctors. Clinical supervisors were more likely than social supervisors to remain unaware of the unobtrusive patients who had ceased and were incident free. Even using the most conservative figures, there was no difference in outcomes for those who had ceased. Doubts have been expressed earlier about the accuracy of information about a number of other patients reported to be on medication, often oral or prescribed by a family doctor, who were also incident free; if only a few of these were added to the figures in Table 4.47 the significance and power of the association would be increased in the opposite direction to that anticipated by doctors.

Table 4.47
Patients ceasing medication by postdischarge incidents (N159)

	Incidents	
	None	Any
Still taking major tranquillisers	47 (44%)	60 (56%)
Ceased medication (including 7 patients conflicting data plus 12 others rarely attending for medication)	33 (67%)	19 (33%)

$$x^2=4.59, \text{df } 1, \text{p}<.025; \text{phi } .17$$

Publicity given to relapses after cessation of medication may adversely affect other patients if it persuades doctors not to attempt reduction or cessation. This would have been unjustified in half the cases in this study about whose cessation of medication there was little doubt, probably in rather more. The situation is similar to the effects upon the discharge of other patients of media publicity given to the relatively rare serious reoffence by a patient in the community. However, if cessation of medication is prescribed, it would seem to be prudent for the supervisor to see the patient during the period when medication is being withdrawn rather more frequently than appeared to be usual, see the section on supervision in Chapter Five.

Marital status

Patients who had ever been married (longterm cohabitation included) were more likely to be well integrated than those who had never married, although the strengths of significant associations with incident scores were weak (none greater than Cramer's V .14). It is difficult to attempt to interpret any causality here. It may be that men who married had more ability to conform to social norms or had superior social skills than the single, although supervisors and others generally thought that marriage after discharge was itself a stabilising factor.

There were, however, significant and strong associations between patients' marriage after discharge and criminal incidents (p<.002, Cramer's V .30; similar figures for weighted criminal incidents). These patients were predominantly younger and psychopathic and on

84

both these counts more likely to be involved in criminal incidents than men married before admission. The unlikely association of criminality with marriage per se may also be discounted in view of the trend towards better scores for integration for all those married after discharge. As might be expected from a representative sample of marriages, a few were disasters and some were very successful. Some extremely unpromising marriages proved successful despite the anxieties of supervisors. Doctors attributed the success of some patients entirely to the influence of their wives; other patients acquired a sense of purpose in life and obvious satisfaction from caring for wives who were dependent upon them in various ways. The balance of the evidence suggests that most marriages were beneficial for the patient and that supervisors were no better at predicting success or failure than patients.

Summary

Preadmission history was a powerful factor affecting diagnosis, and diagnosis was very influential in shaping postdischarge careers. The patients most likely to reoffend were those with a drinking problem, those least likely to do so were patients with admission offences of homicide. Surprisingly, neither Restriction Orders nor lengths of stay in hospital were associated with better outcomes for patients, and long stays appeared to be detrimental for psychopaths. Nonwhite patients were atypical, considering their predominant diagnoses as schizophrenic. Despite evidence of less hospital treatment and more police harrassment than other patients with similar characteristics, nonwhites' postdischarge careers were more successful than might have been expected. Cessation of medication was not associated with poorer outcomes, rather the reverse. Marriage after discharge was associated with successful reintegration, once the associations with criminal involvement were discounted on other grounds.

5 Environmental factors associated with reintegration

Introduction

Doctors who expressed interest in the outcome of research were mostly concerned with patient characteristics discussed in Chapter Four. Which type of offender, which diagnostic categories, what age group, were most at risk? How soon were patients discharged, and did they continue to stay in hospital, or on medication? Did Restriction Orders help in the process of integration? The findings suggest that the importance of patient characteristics lay mainly in their influence on the kind of rehabilitation which patients received after discharge, with one major exception, problem drinking.

Doctors' primary interest is in the individual patient whom they are treating (see DHSS, 1978). This perspective occasionally led to conflict with social supervisors or with government departments, see pages 37-39. It may also have been responsible for some attitudes towards families discussed on pages 27 and 28, and for some problems associated with transfer of supervision considered later in this chapter. Some doctors interviewed took a broader view, expressing concern about public safety or that no family therapy had been available to patients and their families before discharge from the Special Hospital. (No reliable data are available about treatment in the Special Hospital for patients included in this study and this was not investigated in the project reported here; the situation is described briefly on pages 2 and 3). A few NHS hospitals employed psychologists who specialised in rehabilitation of patients before discharge, almost entirely long stay schizophrenic patients, but it was social supervisors who were principally concerned with environmental factors affecting the patient. From the patient's point of view, these were of prime importance; more than half of those interviewed reported problems concerning employment, a third reported financial problems and a quarter, despite the fact that hospitals found nearly half of all first accommodation, had difficulties over housing. Families and supervisors also formed a supportive network in the environment.

It was possible to investigate some aspects of the relationships between patients and their various helpers, using the repertory grids completed by 145 patients in the community. The characteristics of these 145 did not differ significantly from patients who did not complete grids, except that those refusing tended to be more recently discharged. These findings concerning relationships should therefore also apply to all other patients. Another approach to interaction with official helpers is adopted in the second part of this chapter where incident measures are used to examine the association between reintegration and supervision, and between reintegration and various other environmental factors including different kinds of accommodation, employment, 'at risk' situations and disclosure of Special Hospital background. Insights acquired from the grid analysis as well as other material discussed in earlier chapters are used to assist in the interpretation of incident measures.

Relationships with 'official' and 'unofficial' helpers

It was argued in Chapter Two (and in more detail in Appendix One) that the sevenfold repertory grid measure of integration accurately represented relative levels of integration into the community of Special Hospital patients. The grid was also designed to examine relationships, especially those thought to involve 'rapport' and 'emotional involvement'.

Rapport

Attachment theory suggests that perceived rapport with another person is essential for the wellbeing of any normal person and is also likely to be associated with high self esteem. Mackie (1981) reviewed the literature; Henderson (1974, 1977, 1978) and Brown and Harris (1978) provided empirical evidence which supports the theory. Theories and empirical evidence concerning shared attitudes, changes of attitude or reinforcement of attitudes suggest that such rapport, accompanied by liking and indicated by perceived similarity, is also important for shared understandings of the world, see for example, Byrne (1962, 1971); Byrne and Nelson (1965); Duck and Craig (1978); Kelman (1966); Newcomb (1961). Such shared understandings would be desirable in relationships intended to foster and maintain approved attitudes towards independence and rulebreaking which supervisors and others thought desirable in patients. Better outcomes had been reported for clients in an earlier study by the author where social workers adopted fraternal rather than authoritarian approaches (Norris, 1979). Studies of psychotherapy, for example those reviewed by Bergin and Strupp (1972), also suggest that the relationship between patient and helper, rather than technical skills, is associated with therapeutic benefit to patients whose illnesses are not acute.

In this study it was hypothesised that perceived similarity between patients and 'official helpers', that is doctors and social supervisors, would be associated with high scores for integration. Details of the way in which the repertory grid was used to identify perceived similarity are given in Appendix One. There was, incidentally, no indication that this perception was affected by patients' age or social class.

Emotional involvement

Studies by Brown, Monck, Carstairs and Wing (1962), Brown, Birley and Wing (1972), Leff (1976), Leff and Vaughn (1981), and Vaughn and Leff (1976a, 1976b) demonstrated an association between relapse in psychiatric patients and close contact with an 'emotionally involved' relative. Leff, Kuipers, Berkowitz, Eberlen-Vries and Sturgeon (1982) provided evidence of a causal relationship. 'Emotional involvement' was mostly manifested as expressed emotion (EE) for which a measure was devised by Vaughn and Leff (1976a). Other aspects, relatively infrequent according to Leff, were not investigated in the present study. Critical comments were the most reliable indicators of expressed emotion in the studies cited.

Constraints upon time prevented the use of Vaughn and Leff's measure, training in EE assessment being 'long and arduous' according to Leff. It seemed reasonable to suppose that the patient's own perception of criticism, regardless of accuracy, would be the principal mediating factor in its effect. A construct 'often criticises me/doesn't criticise me' was used to indicate the patient's perception of relative levels of criticism by people in his network of relationships. (Because this construct was omitted from some grids collected early in the project this material was available for 131 and not 145 patients). The construct was 'important' for 80 per cent of patients, using weighting on the first three principal components as an indicator of importance (see Appendix One).

Information about frequency of contact with people with whom patients lived was obtained either from questions asked when the grid was completed or from other data collected from documentary sources and interviews. When the patient attended hospital daily, or if he or any of the other people concerned were in full time employment, the amount of contact was assumed to be reduced. In the studies cited above, 35 contact hours per week was the critical length of time affecting relapse. It was hypothesised that there would be an association between low scores for integration and situations where critical unofficial helpers were in most frequent contact with patients, using 'at risk' scores described in Appendix One. 'Unofficial' helpers included family and friends, see Table 5.1A. The prediction was made with some reservations since the indicator of criticism was relative, the amount of contact was imprecise, and there was no previous evidence that patients diagnosed as psychopathic were affected in the same way as those diagnosed as schizophrenic.

The studies cited investigated the effect which relatives' emotional involvement with patients had upon the process of rehabilitation. 'Empathy' is regarded as a beneficial component of therapeutic relationships (see Rogers, 1951; Truax and Carkhuff, 1967) but professionals are generally warned against over involvement. There is no evidence that EE (expressed emotion) by professionals indicates emotional involvement with patients as EE by relatives does. However, since data were available it seemed worth investigating indicators of rapport and emotional involvement for all those involved with patients to see if (a) rapport (indicated by perceived similarity) or absence of emotional involvement was associated with patient success; and (b) if either factor was associated with any particular category of helper.

Surrogates

Care was taken to avoid any distortion which might arise from the use of surrogates for element roles (see Appendix One for an explanation of element roles which are categories such as 'doctor' or 'female family member' for each of which patients supplied a name). If a patient had no female 'close person', usually a wife or girlfriend, he might name a sister or an acquaintance. All but three per cent of surrogates seemed adequately to fill the element role described; staff in childrens' institutions or teachers, occasionally supplied as surrogate relatives by patients with no families, were regarded as reasonable alternatives; recent employers were amongst the small number of surrogates accepted only because the patient knew no one more apt. All analyses were run with and without surrogates and any differences are reported. However, when specific relationships are mentioned below, only the appropriate nominees are included. 'Mother' refers only to mothers but includes any mother regardless of the element role to which she was nominated, for example happy or disliked person, helper, etc. Relationships of named persons were noted, where for example a 'happy person' was also a family member, so that the maximum use could be made of all elicited material. Although 'close female person' may include mothers, sisters, girlfriends and wives, 'wives' only includes wives or cohabitees.

Patients identifying the 'person who helped me most since I left the Special Hospital' quite often named someone who had already been nominated for another role, a 'close female person' perhaps. That name was retained in the original role but noted to be 'first choice helper'. To avoid duplication of elements in the grid, a second name was elicited as the 'person who helped me most since I left the Special Hospital' but this element was clearly marked 'second choice helper' and treated as a surrogate in analysis. Only 'first choices' are included amongst reported findings concerning the person who helped the patient most after he left the Special Hospital unless the patient said he had helped himself more than anyone else had. In these (13) cases the second choice helper has been included in the analysis as a first choice. Table 5.1A shows the various kinds of people whom patients thought had helped them most. Only in this table are the thirteen second choices shown separately, in brackets after the listed roles, so that the rather interesting grid scores for patients choosing 'self' as first helper can be examined.

Table 5.1A
Patients' first choice helpers (N 145)

Role	Number	Grid scores Low (1–4)	High (5–7)
Self	13 [9%]	2 (15%)	11 (85%)
Official helpers:			
Doctor(3)	17 [12%]	10 (59%)	7 (41%)
Nurse	11 [8%]	6 (55%)	5 (45%)
Hostel warden	8 [6%]	4 (50%)	4 (50%)
Social supervisor(1)	36 [25%]	15 (42%)	21 (58%)
Unofficial helpers: (close relative)			
Wife(1)	14 [10%]	9 (64%)	5 (36%)
Mother	11 [8%]	8 (73%)	3 (27%)
Father(2)	2 [1%]	1 (50%)	1 (50%)
Sibling	6 [4%]	4 (67%)	2 (33%)
Unofficial helpers: (not close)			
Other relative	6 [3%]	2 (33%)	4 (67%)
Friend(4)	13 [9%]	7 (54%)	6 (46%)
Church member	3 [2%]	– (–)	3 (100%)
Landlady	3 [2%]	1 (33%)	2 (67%)
Other or unknown(2)	2 [1%]	1 (50%)	1 (50%)
Total	145 [100%]	70 (48%)	75 (52%)

Social supervisors in Tables 5.1A and B include only social workers and probation officers. Church members include one Quaker, one minister and one vicar. 'Other' helpers include an employer and acquaintances.

Table 5.1B summarises the details in Table 5.1A. The significant relationship between the four categories of helpers and grid scores is entirely attributable to 'self'. There is no significant difference between the other three groups when second choice helpers are excluded.

Table 5.1B
Data in Table 5.1A collapsed to major helping categories (N 145)

Role	Number	Grid scores Low(0-3)	High(4-7)
Self	13 [9%]	2 (15%)	11 (85%)
Official helpers	72 [50%]	35 (49%)	37 (51%)
Unofficial helpers: (close relative)	33 [23%]	22 (67%)	11 (33%)
Unofficial helpers: (not close relatives)	27 [19%]	11 (41%)	16 (59%)

$$x^2=10.72, \text{ df } 3, \text{ p} < .025, \text{ Cramer's V } .23$$

In the course of eliciting names for element roles it was necessary (for methodological reasons concerning representativeness of elements) to obtain at least one nominee, 'someone I dislike', about whose attributes the respondent had less than positive feelings. Almost a fifth of patients objected to making this nomination and the surrogate 'someone I feel sorry for' was accepted. No similar objections were made in earlier studies using this grid form and none seem to be recorded in the literature. Moreover, 68 per cent of patients refused to identify the disliked person or person they felt sorry for. Of the 46 patients (32 per cent) who did give names, fifteen named relatives, of whom six were in-laws; ten (22 per cent) named doctors, half being Special Hospital doctors of whom one was named by three different patients. Even when the patient professed difficulty in finding a nominee, the person finally selected was almost always 'important' in the patient's construct world (see Appendix One) and other analysis of persons the patient felt sorry for did not differ from that for disliked persons.

Importance of element roles to patients

An unanticipated finding was that 'disliked persons' were of paramount importance to about 80 per cent of patients, see Table 5.2. Patients' marked reluctance to admit dislike or name the person disliked suggests that many of them felt compelled to conceal strong negative feelings. The object of suppressed or repressed dislike may well be significant in a patient's construct world.

Table 5.2 shows the various elements ranked by their importance to patients (see Appendix One for an explanation of the way this table and those following were composed). 'First choice helper' includes people who also appear in other roles. Some 'happy' or 'disliked' people who were also relatives, friends, doctors or supervisors are included in the appropriate group as well as amongst the 'happy', etc. Although the same element may appear more than once for each of the 145 patients in the table this duplication does not affect the analysis which follows. However, the total number of patients and percentage in Tables 5.2, 5.3, 5.4 and 5.9 must greatly exceed 145 and 100 per cent since these tables merely list the number of patients for whom these elements, including duplicates, appeared in the first two (or three in Table 5.9) ranks of the analysis described in Appendix One. It is the rank order based on the percentage of all patients who perceived elements in this light (not the percentage of elements) which is of importance for these particular analyses.

Table 5.2
Elements ranked by importance to patients

Element	Number	Percent (of 145)
Disliked person	115	79%*
Ditto, excluding surrogates	95	79%*
Doctor	39	27%
First choice person who helped most since leaving S.H.	30	21%
Close female person	26	18%
Family member (male)	24	17%
Happy person	21	14%
Family member (female)	19	13%
Best (male) friend	18	12%
Social supervisor	13	9%

* Percentage of 120 disliked persons, excluding surrogates, shown because of the large number of surrogates for this element. Comments are made under further tables only where percentages differ for surrogates.

Doctors and first choice helpers together formed a group as important as disliked persons, but their importance was not necessarily equated with admiration or positive regard.

Although social supervisors formed by far the highest proportion of first choice helpers, especially if wardens and nurses who were formally supervising are included, they were on the whole relatively

92

unimportant compared to other people in the patients' lives. This may be the result of frequent changes of social supervisor, already reported in Chapter Three. 25 per cent of patients had three or more social supervisors. Only eight per cent had three or more doctors, even when registrars are included, but 30 per cent of patients saw their doctors rarely if ever, so doctors' importance may have been due to the predominant role they were thought to play in recommending release from conditions of discharge or recall to Special Hospitals.

There was no relationship between importance to the patient of any element role and high (5-7) or low (1-4) grid scores for integration. (This is the dichotomy which gives roughly equal distribution of patients into two groups of high and low scorers, see page 13, always used unless otherwise stated).

Ideal attributes

Nor was there any relationship between scores for integration and patients' perceptions of particular kinds of persons with ideal attributes. Table 5.3 shows element roles perceived as most like the patient's 'ideal self', that is with qualities which the patient thought desirable.

Table 5.3
Elements most like 'ideal self'

Element	Number	Percent (of 145)
First choice helper	71	49%
Close female person	44	30%
Doctor	36	25%
Best (male) friend	33	23%
Family member (female)	30	21%
Social supervisor	27	19%
Happy person	26	18%
Family member (male)	26	18%
Disliked person	6	4%

First choice helpers were most often seen as having ideal qualities, followed by 'close female person', usually wives but sometimes mothers. Four per cent of disliked people were seen as having the most ideal qualities of all people in patients' networks of relationships.

Thus neither the importance of helpers to a patient nor their admirable attributes was associated with integration.

Perceived similarity

Table 5.4 overleaf shows the numbers of patients perceiving various elements as most like themselves.

Table 5.4
Elements most like patients' 'self'

Element	Number	Percent (of 145)
First choice helper	51	35%
Close female person	50	34%
Best (male) friend	46	32%
Family member (female)	37	26%
Happy person	29	19%
Disliked person	25	17%
Family member (male)	21	15%
Doctor	19	13%
Social supervisor	18	12%

In Table 5.4 surrogates for 'close female person' supplied by patients with no women friends did differ from genuine wives and cohabitees. Surrogates all appeared in the last four ranks, less like the patient.

The majority of patients perceived themselves as dissimilar to the person they disliked, though for 17 per cent the disliked person appeared as one of the two elements most like self. The fact that all these 17 per cent of patients had poor self esteem suggests that they did not much like themselves either and it is probable that the ability to like others depends on accepting and valuing self. Liking is not, of course, necessarily associated with perceived similarity. There is evidence that similarity can be threatening in some circumstances. This has been found to be the case when similarity was perceived with persons known to be mentally ill (Novak and Lerner, 1968); many patients in the present study disliked persons who were or had been fellow patients.

Perceived similarity with a supervisor does not, however, merely indicate that a patient who already had reasonable self esteem shared socially acceptable attitudes with his supervisor. It is, moreover, arguable that rapport (indicated by perceived similarity combined, it seems, with a modicum of self esteem if the relationship is to include liking) is the causal factor in any association found between the establishment of rapport and successful reintegration, although the latter is measured by the grid which includes self esteem as an indicator. The grid measures change, see Appendix One, and there is also evidence that a person with low self esteem is more likely to respond positively to expressed appreciation or liking (Dittes, 1959; Walster, 1965). Successful efforts made by a supervisor to establish rapport (Berscheid and Walster, 1969, review the effects of various kinds of positive evaluation in generating liking) would, according to Rogers (1951), increase a patient's self esteem. For patients with low self esteem such an increase would be a necessary precursor to the establishment of a relationship (indicated by perceived similarity and accompanied by liking) which is initiated by the supervisor and which fosters socially approved attitudes in all patients. Increases in self esteem and enhancements of socially approved attitudes after leaving the Special Hospital would be measured by the grid; if the attitudes and esteem existed before supervision no change would be recorded. It should perhaps also be noted that only one first choice helper was also a disliked person and that none of the ten doctors (and one probation officer) who were also disliked persons were currently supervising.

In fact identification with all first choice helpers was associated with high scores for integration, see Table 5.5, although the association was not strong. (First and second ranks were used to smooth any chance oddities in distribution in the first rank, see Appendix One).

Table 5.5
Perceived similarity with first choice helper by grid scores for integration (N 145)

First choice helper	Scores for integration	
	Low	High
Ranked 1st or 2nd for perceived similarity	18 (35%)	33 (65%)
Ranked other than first or second	52 (55%)	42 (45%)

$$\chi^2 = 4.54, \text{ df } 1, \text{ p} < .05, \text{ phi } .18$$

Patients' age, social class and education did not affect these associations, but the kind of helper chosen seemed to be related to perceptions of similarity. More patients (63 per cent of the small number, five out of eight) perceived similarity with wardens named as first choice helpers than with first choice helpers who were doctors (30 per cent of 17), social supervisors (27 per cent of 36) or nurses (10 per cent of the small number, 1 of 11).

Moreover the hypothesis that perceived similarity with official helpers would be associated with high scores for integration was supported, see Tables 5.6 and 5.7 overleaf. There was no such association for any category of unofficial helper. Wives, including cohabitees, were perceived as similar significantly (p<.05) more often than other unofficial helpers but their husbands were no more likely to have higher scores than patients with other unofficial first choice helpers.

The findings suggest that perceived similarity with a doctor or social supervisor does contribute to successful reintegration. Failure to establish rapport or inability to establish therapeutic interaction may in part result from incompatibilities for which neither supervisor nor patient is responsible. In these circumstances benefit to the patient might result from a change of supervisor and it would be possible to monitor increased self esteem, changes in attitude and any greater perception of similarity with a new supervisor by using the grid measure.

Table 5.6
Perceived similarity with doctor by grid scores for integration
(N 145)

Doctor	Scores for integration	
	Low	High
Ranked 1st or 2nd for perceived similarity	5 (23%)	16 (76%)
Ranked other than first or second	65 (52%)	59 (48%)

$$X^2 = 4.70, \text{ df } 1, \text{ } p < .05, \text{ phi } .18$$

Table 5.7
Perceived similarity with social supervisor by grid scores for integration (N 145)

Social supervisor	Scores for integration	
	Low	High
Ranked 1st or 2nd for perceived similarity	7 (27%)	19 (73%)
Ranked other than first or second	63 (53%)	56 (47%)

$$X^2 = 5.79, \text{ df } 1, \text{ } p < .025, \text{ phi } .20$$

Although perceived similarity with an official helper, regardless of the role in the grid to which he or she was assigned by the patient, was associated with higher scores for patient integration, perceived similarity was an insignificant factor when an unofficial helper was a patient's first choice. Emotional involvement therefore seemed likely to account for differences in patient integration associated with different categories of unofficial helper.

Criticism as an indicator of emotional involvement

Despite rather small numbers, there was a significant ($p < .05$) and quite strong association between low scores and patient nomination of close relatives as first choice helpers, see Table 5.8. The definition of 'close relatives' in that table excluded two low scoring patients whose 'other relatives' had a much closer relationship than the degree of kinship indicated and the association may therefore be underestimated. 'Friends' were omitted since it was not possible to distinguish close from not close friends. The association shown in Table 5.8 was thought likely to be related to the hypothesis, see page 89, that there would be an association between low scores for integration and contact with emotionally involved (critical) relatives.

Table 5.8
'Unofficial' helpers by grid scores for patient integration (N 52)

	Scores for integration	
First choice helper	Low	High
Close relatives (wives, parents, sibs)	24 (67%)	12 (33%)
Other relatives, landladies, church members, etc.	5 (31%)	11 (69%)

$$X^2 = 4.29, \text{ df } 1, \text{ p}<.05; \text{ phi } .29$$

Relationships with critical people were then examined, see Table 5.9. The numbers and percentages resulting from the use of two and three ranks (see Appendix One for the details of the process) are both shown below to demonstrate that there is little difference in the ranking of elements produced by either approach.

Table 5.9
Most critical elements (N 131)

Element	Using two ranks		Using three ranks	
	Number	Percent (of 131)	Number	Percent (of 131)
Disliked person	56	43%	60	46%
Family member (male)	42	32%	57	44%
Family member (female)	37	29%	56	43%
Doctor	27	20%	42	32%
First choice helper	26	20%	49	37%
Best (male) friend	24	18%	38	29%
Close (female) person	21	16%	36	27%
Social supervisor	17	12%	34	26%
Happy person	13	10%	21	16%

The main groups of element roles were considered in turn, first official helpers, then unofficial helpers including the close relatives whose emotional involvement was expected to account for the differences in integration. Because of the importance of investigating these relationships only current supervisors were included in the analysis which follows and any surrogates were excluded, but the analysis was based on the use of three ranks, to prevent the data being swamped with 'disliked persons' who predominated in the first two ranks.

Official helpers: doctors

28 per cent (37, excluding 5 surrogates or not currently supervising) of patients who had completed grids perceived their doctor as critical, suggesting emotional involvement if this can be measured in the same way for official helpers as for relatives. Some support for such an interpretation was found in soft data analysis of interview material where some doctors who had had lengthy supervisions made comments which in a relative would certainly be regarded as over protective, over involved. There was no association between critical doctors and patient scores for integration.

Official helpers: social supervisors

However, of 21 per cent (27, excluding 7 surrogates or not currently supervising) of patients who perceived their social supervisor as critical, 67 per cent were high scorers, a significant ($p < .025$) relationship in the unexpected direction. Critical people were quite often disliked persons but in four of six cases where a social supervisor was perceived as both most similar and most critical the patient was a high scorer. Other factors may be involved and the numbers are small but there is no evidence here to support the notion that a degree of emotional detachment is of benefit to the client.

Other element roles

Fathers were perceived as critical more often than wives, mothers or siblings, and brothers were more critical than sisters, but only patients' children were significantly more critical ($p < .05$) than other relatives or unofficial helpers. There was no association between critical relatives and scores for reintegration, nor did consideration of the degree of contact measured by 'at risk' scores, see Appendix One, affect this analysis.

First choice helpers and criticism

There were, however, significant differences between kinds of critical relatives chosen as first choice helpers. Not a single critical mother and no critical children were first choice helpers, but all six first choice sibling helpers were critical brothers. However, the perception of helpers as critical did not account for the difference in scores in Table 5.8 above between patients whose first choice helpers were close or less close relatives; nor did degree of contact appear to affect these findings. Because of earlier reservations about the lack of evidence that psychopaths were affected by critical relatives, diagnoses were examined.

Diagnoses

Schizophrenic patients were significantly ($p < .05$) more likely to choose doctors as first choice helpers but their scores for integration were not associated with this choice. However, there was a difference between scores for schizophrenics and for psychopaths whose first choice helpers were close relatives, see Table 5.10.

Table 5.10
Close relatives and other unofficial helpers by scores for integration, controlled for diagnosis (N 119)

	Score for integration			
	Psychopaths		Schizophrenics	
First choice helpers	Low	High	Low	High
Close relatives	10 (71%)	4 (29%)	7 (37%)	12 (63%)
All other unofficial helpers	15 (37%)	26 (63%)	22 (49%)	23 (51%)

X^2=3.8 (3.84 required for p<.05), df 1; phi .26: not significant

This Table shows a distribution which borders on statistical significance, for associations between low scores for integration and a diagnosis of psychopathy (not schizophrenia as anticipated) when first choice helpers were close relatives. The association was not because those schizophrenic patients who had lived with close relatives had already relapsed and been readmitted to hospital, since no more patients with 'at risk scores', see Appendix One, were readmitted than others. An alternative explanation was supported by the evidence that patients who had been diagnosed as psychopaths were significantly (p<.025) more likely to be regarded as 'doing well' than those diagnosed as schizophrenic. It has already been argued that doctors and social supervisors were disinclined to regard psychopaths as ill. If such patients were finding it difficult to cope they would be less likely to be readmitted to hospital and more likely to seek support from a relative. The association between low scores and care by close relatives of psychopaths may not be causal: it may indicate lack of support from official sources for psychopathic patients, further evidence of the social consequences of diagnosis.

Summary of relationships with helpers

The hypothesis that rapport, indicated by perceived similarity, would be associated with better integration was supported but for official helpers only, a finding with implications for supervisory relationships.

The hypothesis that patients who perceived their helpers as critical would be less well integrated was not sustained. An unanticipated finding was that it was psychopathic and not schizophrenic patients whose low scores were significantly associated with first choice for helper of a close relative. It is very probable that Special Hospital patients, many of whom waited for a very long time for discharge, were less ill than the schizophrenics in the studies on which this hypothesis was based. However, it seemed that admission diagnoses were influential in this aspect of postdischarge careers.

Employment

Being able to find employment quickly was not a factor associated with early discharge from NHS hospitals. 57 per cent of those staying more than a year and 43 per cent of those staying less than a year obtained employment within six months after discharge, a situation which would have been reversed if ability to find work influenced discharge.

Since employment was a factor associated with several incident and grid measures it might be useful to summarise these in full as a reminder of the variety of measures used. (Incident measures were discussed earlier, see page 50). Incidents were negatively associated and grid measures positively associated with 'working at time of interview'. All incident measures were trichotomised, and grid scores dichotomised, giving a series of six three by two tables for incidents and nine two by two tables for grids.

The complete set of significance levels and associations for these fifteen tables of measures and 'working at time of interview' can be summarised as follows (see page 11 for a list of grid aspects):

Working by:	x^2	df	sig.level	phi C.V
(i) Psychiatric incidents (frequency)	24.88	2	<.001	.31
(ii) Psychiatric incidents (weighted)	27.71	2	<.001	.33
(iii) Criminal incidents (frequency)	8.65	2	<.01	.18
(iv) Criminal incidents (weighted)	11.14	2	<.003	.21
(v) All incidents (frequency)	28.79	2	<.001	.34
(vi) All incidents (weighted)	29.33	2	<.001	.34
(vii) Grid score 1 (see Table 2.4)	3.35	1	<.07 *	.16
(viii) Grid score 2 (see Table 2.4)			not significant	
(ix) Aspect 1 self esteem			not significant	
(x) Aspect 2 rulebreaking aspiration			not significant	
(xi) Aspect 3 rulebreaking selfpercept	3.23	1	<.07 *	.15
(xii) Aspect 4 less rulebreak'g since SH			not significant	
(xiii) Aspect 5 independence aspiration			not significant	
(xiv) Aspect 6 independence selfpercept	2.58	1	<.10 *	.14
(xv) Aspect 7 more independent since SH	3.20	1	<.07 *	.16

*suggestive not significant

The positive associations of employment with success measured by the grid were weak and the negative associations of employment with incidents, that is that those working were less likely to have been involved, were strong. The weaker association between working and not being involved in criminal (rather than psychiatric) incidents was not, as at first thought possible, the logical consequence of the greater difficulty of maintaining employment for patients involved in numerous psychiatric hospital admissions since those involved in criminal activities had similar problems, see 'Diagnosis and employment' in Chapter Four. However, the strength of all associations may be an artefact of the greater difficulty of maintaining employment when involved in incidents, rather than any indication that employment prevents such involvement.

This interpretation is supported by the fact that employment was not, as would be expected if it was contributing to successful reintegration, associated with increased self esteem and it was very weakly associated with other positive aspects measured by the grid. This may be because of the unsatisfactory nature of employment available to many patients, see page 31.

Accommodation

Although hostels were the placement many doctors thought most suitable for patients after discharge, patients who had lived in hostels were more likely than those discharged to other accommodation to be involved in both criminal and psychiatric incidents, see Table 5.11, though the associations were weak and not always significant.

Table 5.11
Residence in hostel or other accommodation by criminal and psychiatric incidents (N 294)

	Criminal incidents		Psychiatric incidents	
	None	Any	None	Any
Hostel	72 (65%)	38 (35%)	65 (59%)	45 (41%)
Other accommodation	142 (77%)	42 (23%)	127 (69%)	57 (31%)

X^2= 4.77, df 1, p<.03; phi .13 : X^2= 3.00, suggestive not sig.

There were some differences in the proportions of patients with different admission offences placed in hostels or other accommodation, see Table 5.12 overleaf, but for all types of offenders there was a similar trend for hostel residence to be associated with recidivism and relapse.

Table 5.12
Admission offence by hostel or other accommodation (N294)

Offence	Hostel	Other
Homicide and attempted homicide	30 (35%)	55 (65%)
Sexual	16 (52%)	15 (48%)
Arson	20 (53%)	18 (47%)
Assault	32 (34%)	63 (66%)
Acquisitive	7 (28%)	18 (72%)
Other	5 (25%)	15 (75%)

x^2=9.42, df 5, suggestive not significant: Cramer's V .18

A rather greater proportion of psychopaths than schizophrenics was discharged to hostels, although almost equal numbers of each diagnostic group would then be found in hostels, see Table 5.13.

Table 5.13
To whom discharged by diagnosis (N 252)

	Psychopathic	Schizophrenic
Alone or with wife	9 (20%) [9%]	36 (80%) [24%]
Parents	32 (42%) [32%]	44 (58%) [29%]
Close relatives or friends	7 (25%) [7%]	21 (75%) [14%]
Hostel residents, few others	52 (50%) [52%]	51 (50%) [34%]

x^2=15.01, df 3, p<.005; Cramer's V .24

Controlling Table 5.11 for diagnosis showed a rather similar pattern of criminal offences for psychopaths and schizophrenics as for all patients, though the distributions were not significant, see Table 5.14. A similar pattern of relapses was shown for both diagnostic groups but the association with relapse and hostel residence was stronger for psychopaths, verging on significance, see Table 5.15 opposite. (Some data on patients with diagnoses other than the two major categories are omitted from these Tables, accounting for the reduction in numbers from Table 5.11).

Table 5.14
Hostel or other accommodation by criminal incidents, controlled for diagnosis (N 260)

	Psychopaths Incidents		Schizophrenics Incidents	
	None	Any	None	Any
Hostel	29 (58%)	21 (42%)	36 (71%)	15 (29%)
Other accommodation	38 (70%)	16 (30%)	83 (79%)	22 (21%)

Table 5.15
Hostel or other accommodation by psychiatric incidents, controlled
for diagnosis (N 260)

	Psychopaths Incidents		Schizophrenics Incidents	
	None	Any	None	Any
Hostel	33 (66%)	17 (34%)	26 (51%)	25 (49%)
Other accommodation	44 (81%)	10 (18%)	65 (62%)	40 (38%)

x^2=3.24, df 1, suggestive not significant, phi .18: not significant

However, age was also a factor of some consequence. Equal proportions of all age groups went to hostels but when Table 5.11 was controlled for age at discharge it was apparent that it was the younger age group which accounted for the high proportion of criminal offences committed by patients who had been in hostels, see Table 5.16. It was the association of youth with psychopathy and greater age with schizophrenia which largely accounted for the apparent association of diagnoses with different kinds of deviant behaviour by hostel residents.

Table 5.16
Hostel or other accommodation by criminal incidents, controlled for
age at discharge (N 294)

	Age 40 and under Incidents		Age 41 and over Incidents	
	None	Any	None	Any
Hostel	44 (56%)	35 (44%)	28 (90%)	3 (10%)
Other accommodation	90 (73%)	34 (27%)	52 (87%)	8 (13%)

x^2=6.13, df 1, p<.025; phi .17

The conclusion is that younger psychopaths were more likely to commit criminal offences when discharged to hostels. Older men regardless of diagnosis were less likely to be involved in deviant behaviour, in keeping with the general trend in criminal statistics. There was a trend, quite marked amongst psychopaths, for a higher proportion of hostel residents than other patients to relapse.

It will be recalled that parents, see Table 3.12, despite the misgivings of doctors and of studies concerning the effect of family life upon the mentally ill, were very supportive to patients. Only 19 parents refused to accommodate their son because of a poor family relationship. It might be thought that parents only accommodated patients with better prognoses, and that this accounted for fewer incidents for patients living with parents. This was not the case.

Some patients were discharged to, or moved to live with, parents against the advice of their doctor, because there was no alternative. In fact 16 per cent of patients discharged to parents returned to a disorganised family and another eight returned to parents after the breakdown of their own marriage. A quarter of patients who completed grids named close relatives as first choice helpers and 67 per cent of these had low scores for integration, see Table 5.1B. Psychopaths were more likely than schizophrenics to have low scores when living with relatives, see Table 5.10, and it has already been noted that psychopaths might return to parents quite soon after their discharge to a hostel.

Roughly the same proportion of patients remained with parents as remained in a hostel throughout the research period, suggesting that such placements were equally stable. Nor did placement with parents inhibit development of independent social relationships; all but one of the 75 per cent of these patients who subsequently left home did so because they married or moved to live with a cohabitee.

A patient discharged to parents may be in a more favourable environment than if he were given a hostel placement. However, according to 'soft data' analysis, parents were often discouraged from taking too active an interest in their son whilst he was in Broadmoor; letters to doctors remained unanswered for long periods and requests for interviews were refused or ignored. Some parents were undoubtedly a great nuisance to hospital staff and only ceased pestering any person likely to assist if their persistence created difficulties for the patient. Not all were helpful to their sons after discharge. Nevertheless parents were a major source of support for many patients in the immediate postdischarge period and sometimes for years afterwards; this was despite the parents' age, illness and incapacity and also sometimes the illness and incapacity of the patient, this 'cuckoo in the nest', as a supervisor described one man whose family were making heroic efforts to cope. Some suggestions are made in Chapter Seven for making more fruitful use of parental concern.

Supervision

Lengths of supervision

Longer social and medical supervisions were associated with more frequent and more severe relapse. Quality of supervision, indicated by frequency of contact and few changes of supervisor, is discussed later in this section.

Longer social supervisions when divided into four categories (less than a year, 1 > 2 years, 2 > 4 years, and 4 or more years) were significantly but rather weakly associated with involvement in (i) more frequent and (ii) more serious (weighted) psychiatric incidents and (vi) all serious incidents (p<.025, Cramer's V .19; p<.05, Cramer's V .17; and p<.04, Cramer's V .18 respectively; the bracketed numbers (i), (ii) and (vi) are reminders of the incident tables listed on page 50). How should this be interpreted? It had nothing to do with Restriction Orders, since there was no difference in length of social supervisions for restricted and unrestricted patients.

Just over half of those 219 patients for whom details of lengths of supervision were known had two or more years of social supervision. Frequency of involvement in psychiatric or criminal incidents seemed to support the view that patients whose life style was deviant had longer supervision, see Tables 5.17 and 5.18, although the whole purpose, particularly of statutory supervision, must surely be to prevent deviant behaviour. The two tables have been simplified to facilitate comparisons by collapsing the four periods described above to two and showing only percentages.

Table 5.17
Long and short social supervisions by percentage frequency and seriousness of psychiatric incidents (N 219)

Length	Psychiatric incidents			Weighted incidents		
	Nil	1	2+	Nil	1–2	3–22
Less than two years	[50%]	[46%]	[28%]	[49%]	[36%]	[42%]
Two or more years	[50%]	[54%]	[72%]	[51%]	[64%]	[58%]

Table 5.18
Long and short social supervisions by percentage frequency and seriousness of criminal incidents (N 219)

Length	Criminal incidents			Weighted incidents		
	Nil	1	2+	Nil	1–2	3–11
Less than two years	[48%]	[34%]	[48%]	[48%]	[25%]	[48%]
Two or more years	[52%]	[66%]	[52%]	[52%]	[75%]	[52%]

All four sections of these tabulations show similar percentages of patients remaining incident free whether supervision was long or short. However, the middle columns in each of the four sections of the tables above demonstrate the distributions which account for the significant associations in the full tabulations. That is, the percentage of deviant behaviour increases with length of supervision. In the table for frequency of psychiatric incidents, figures in the third column also support the argument. The reason that the other three tables fail to show a similar pattern is because very serious incidents (or more than one criminal incident) almost inevitably led to an abrupt termination of supervision when the patient was recalled, sent to prison or, in the event of suicide, died.

When those 52 patients whose formal medical supervision lapsed before absolute discharge were added to those 56 whose supervisions were terminated formally, similar patterns for lengths of supervision and involvement in incidents were observed. The quarter of supervisions which ended within two years were generally without incident but none were ended before two years for patients involved in more than one psychiatric incident. Longer formal medical supervisions were also positively associated with patient involvement in serious criminal incidents ($p<.01$); this is largely the result of redefining deviant behaviour as criminal rather than 'sick' when treatment seemed unavailing and the situation is discussed in more detail in Chapter Seven.

For 37 informal medical supervisions the situation was reversed and because of the nature of these supervisions the lengths of time were divided into 'less than three months', 'three months and less than two years' and 'two or more years'. Very brief informal supervisions were significantly and strongly associated with serious incidents ($p<.02$, Cramer's V .44) some of which involved drinking. Informal medical supervision was the only kind of supervision which was more likely to continue longer for patients not involved in incidents. Although bureaucratic requirements made restrictions unpopular, see pages 37-38 and 64, it does seem that if mandatory supervision was abandoned some patients apparently in need of help might find it more difficult to obtain psychiatric treatment. There was a steady accumulation of evidence that patients who were young, psychopathic, nonwhite or problem drinkers received less assistance than those who were perceived as sick but who were also easier to help, readily accepted assistance and were very little trouble.

There was also no association between any grid measure and length of supervision, so that no positive effects related merely to lengths of supervision could be found. Was there any benefit in continuing these supervisions, which many patients and supervisors found burdensome? It might be argued that if supervision had ceased earlier more of those patients with long supervisions who were incident free might have offended or relapsed. There was one area, namely psychiatric supervision, where the argument that lengthy treatment was prophylactic could be tested; the relationship of reoffending and hospital readmissions was therefore examined.

Patients with psychiatric supervision had significantly ($p<.04$) more NHS hospital readmissions than those without supervision (39 per cent and 24 per cent respectively, though the association was surprisingly weak, phi .11). Doctors sometimes argued that these admissions were not a sign of relapse but were prophylactic. If that were generally the case it should be found that a smaller proportion of patients who had the benefit of psychiatric supervision and were admitted to hospital committed offences than those who were not admitted. The reverse was the case, at a strong and significant level (p<.001; phi .25). 62 per cent of supervised patients admitted had already committed an offence; 31 per cent of those not admitted had committed an offence. (An even lower percentage of patients with more than one offence were not admitted to hospital because they went to prison). A supporter of the prophylactic view of admission might argue that those patients admitted might have committed even more offences if not admitted; however, offences preceded admission by a mean length of about 20 months in almost all instances. The time scale strongly suggests that admission was a last resort rather than an early preventative measure.

There is no evidence here that lengthy postdischarge social or medical supervision prevents recidivism. The patterns of supervision do not show that deviant behaviour is changed by lengthy supervision. What were the effects of other aspects of supervision, such as frequency of contact, continuity of care and medication?

Frequency of contact

For social supervisors, frequency of contact was dichotomised at the point which gave the most equal division of patients (for whom this information was available) into two groups, those with frequent contact, which was therefore defined as three weekly or more often, and those whose contact with their supervisors was less frequent. Using this dichotomy and the usual categories of incident scores, the associations below between frequent contact with (N 150) social supervisors and more involvement in incidents were found.

Frequency (social supervision) by:	x^2	df	sig.level	phi C.V
(i) Psychiatric incidents (frequency)	10.14	2	<.006	.26
(ii) Psychiatric incidents (weighted)	5.37	2	<.01	.25
(iii) Criminal incidents (frequency)	5.24	2	<.07*	.19
(iv) Criminal incidents (weighted)			not significant	
(v) All incidents (frequency)	8.70	2	<.01	.24
(vi) All incidents (weighted)	9.24	2	<.01	.25
(vii) Grid score 1 (see Table 2.4)	4.5	1	<.03	.20
(viii) Grid score 2 (see Table 2.4)	7.54	1	<.006	.26
(ix) Aspect 1 self esteem			not significant	
(x) Aspect 2 rulebreaking aspiration	4.73	1	<.02	.22
(xi) Aspect 3 rulebreaking selfpercept			not significant	
(xii) Aspect 4 less rulebreak'g since SH	3.89	1	<.05	.18
(xiii) Aspect 5 independence aspiration			not significant	
(xiv) Aspect 6 independence selfpercept	2.8	1	<.09*	.16
(xv) Aspect 7 more independent since SH			not significant	

*suggestive not significant

There were quite strong associations between frequent contact and low scores for integration, and some associations between frequent contact and those aspects which were least desired, more rulebreaking, less independence.

The relationships between frequency of contact and involvement in incidents were similar to those for lengths of supervision although the associations were rather stronger. The same conclusion was reached, that is that frequency of contact, like length of supervision, is a response to patient behaviour and does not markedly affect it.

Grid findings support the argument. Social supervisors 'often' saw 80 per cent of those with low scores for integration, 58 per cent of those with high scores. Those clients seen less often were more likely (though not always significantly so) to have increased self esteem, aspirations not to be rulebreaking, self percepts as nonrulebreaking, as less rulebreaking than at discharge and as being independent. It might be argued that the better integrated need less frequent supervisory contact since they had benefited from earlier and more frequent contact. It was true that there was a considerable decrease in frequency of contact over time. If earlier frequent contact had benefited clients then longer periods of supervision should be associated with high scores; but the reverse was found as described in the preceding section.

Frequency of contact was trichotomised for medical supervisors because of the high proportion (one third) of active patients who never or rarely saw their doctor. Another 40 per cent were seen between one and four times a year and 28 per cent more frequently. Associations between frequent contact by psychiatrists and psychiatric incidents were strong:

Frequency (medical supervision) by:	x^2	df	sig.level	phi C.V
(i) Psychiatric incidents (frequency)	22.78	4	<.001	.30
(ii) Psychiatric incidents (weighted)	20.78	4	<.001	.29
(iii) Criminal incidents (frequency)			not significant	
(iv) Criminal incidents (weighted)			not significant	
(v) All incidents (frequency)	11.11	4	<.02	.21
(vi) All incidents (weighted)	7.35		not significant	.17

Again the relationship shows, not that frequent supervision reduced the number of incidents in which patients were involved, but that the less frequent the contact the less likely the patient was to be involved in psychiatric incidents. Once more it is difficult to argue that the situation is the result of earlier frequent contact producing less deviant behaviour in patients over time, since longer medical supervisions were also associated with more frequent and more serious incidents.

The lack of any association between frequent doctor/patient contact and criminal incidents is partly due to the fact that doctors were far more likely to be treating schizophrenics than psychopaths, see Tables 4.7 and 4.8. Half of all psychopathic patients with medical supervision never or rarely saw their doctor. The deviant behaviour of patients known to be having medical treatment is more likely to be perceived as symptomatic of illness than as criminal; there was evidence of less frequent police contact with schizophrenics, see Table 4.9. Doctors also saw significantly more older patients (p<.001; Cramer's V .37), partly because of the association between age and diagnosis. Just under half of all patients aged 35 or less at discharge were never or rarely seen by their doctor. Older patients were less likely to be involved in criminal activities and it is improbable that medical supervision had much influence on the behaviour of patients rarely seen. Doctors were sometimes under the impression that their presence 'in the background' did have an effect; one or two patients were however unaware that there was a doctor formally supervising in such instances.

In medical as well as in social supervision there was a suggestive but not significant trend for patients who saw their doctor less frequently to have better grid outcomes. For example, 71 per cent of those who rarely or never saw their doctor had increased self esteem; 65 per cent of those who saw their doctor between 1 and 4 times a year and only 48 per cent of those who saw the doctor frequently had increased self esteem (p<.09; Cramer's V .20).

The associations between deviant behaviour and longer and more frequent medical and social supervision suggest a response to deviant behaviour by the supervising services which matches general public anxiety about Special Hospital patients. There seems to be no evidence of a steady improvement resulting from any positive effects of planned rehabilitation.

Continuity of care

Continuity of care scores, see Appendix One, Table 3, show that 72 per cent of active patients scored 2 or fewer points. A patient who during four years of medical and social supervision had one doctor and two social supervisors would score 7. One who during two years social and medical supervision had no change of supervisor would score 4; if he had had two doctors and one social supervisor he would score 3. Only 28 per cent achieved this rather rudimentary level of continuity and the percentage of very low scores indicates that some unfortunate patients had many changes of supervisor during brief supervisions.

For the purposes of analysis scores were grouped into three categories, see Appendix One. The pattern of associations between frequent and lengthy supervisions and the involvement of the patient in more numerous and grave incidents was repeated. 81 per cent of those with least continuous care were incident free compared to 66 per cent of those with most continuous care, but the associations were extremely weak. Grid findings associated with continuous care also followed the previous pattern; 57 per cent of patients in the group receiving least continuous care compared to 39 per cent of those receiving most continuous care had self percepts as nonrulebreaking.

There were associations between scores for continuity of care and both age and diagnosis. 62 per cent of those aged under 35 at discharge had scores of more than 3 for continuity; only 38 per cent of the older men had such high scores and the difference was significant although the association was not strong (p<.05, Cramer's V .15). It was at first surprising, since psychopaths were unpopular with supervisors, to find that they had significantly more continuity of care. However, it became apparent that there was little difference between percentages of patients with either diagnosis receiving continuous care: amongst low scorers receiving interrupted or discontinuous supervision, 64 per cent were schizophrenic. When the association between continuity and diagnosis was controlled for age it was apparent that this was the important factor. It was only young psychopaths who had 'less interrupted care' presumably resulting from tenuous contact with a doctor who did not terminate (or perhaps was not permitted to terminate) an apparently undemanding supervision. Frequent interruptions to continuity for some schizophrenics probably resulted from their treatment by registrars, who moved often, and to the fact that hospital social workers were less stable in post than other social supervisors, see page 39.

Continuity of care, unlike length and to some extent frequency of contact, is an aspect of supervision unaffected by requirements of Restriction Orders or public opinion. So far as patients are concerned it only reflects the concern of the agency or doctor with their rehabilitation if it is combined with frequency of contact. Continuity may then be genuinely rehabilitatory, permitting the establishment of a relationship which contributes to integration and which is therefore less likely to be terminated by patient misdemeanours. Fostering the rapport found to be associated with reintegration would hardly be possible during brief or discontinuous periods of supervision. Patients found the recital of their past history to a series of supervisors distressing and some consultants specifically stated that for this reason they always saw Special Hospital patients themselves. This was not a universal practice and some nominal supervisors hardly knew the patient. A few social supervisors made a point of arranging joint supervision with a colleague for some time before any change, thus avoiding disruption and the repetition of history. However, when the brevity of much supervision and the infrequency of contact already mentioned are combined with the indication of discontinuity in these scores, it is surprising that any supervisors managed to establish rapport.

Summary of lengths, frequency and continuity of supervision

The pattern of social and medical supervision was similar for lengths, frequency and continuity of care. There was no evidence that these factors affected deviant behaviour and where it was possible to test the claim that medical supervision was prophylactic, evidence appeared to show that it was more often a last resort. On the whole, therefore, care appeared to be a response to patient behaviour rather than a factor in guiding behaviour. Intervention as a result of deviant behaviour would have occurred whether or not there had been statutory supervision. However, it should be recalled that in the earlier sections of this chapter it was shown that the relationship established between patient and supervisor did seem to affect patient integration. There were, therefore, conscientious and skilled supervisors providing effective aftercare for some patients. However, a rather rudimentary service was provided for many of those not seen to be troublesome, especially the psychopathic and those aged 35 or under at discharge. The general pattern of care reported would not facilitate the establishment of rapport which was associated with reintegration.

Transfer problems

Some problems in supervision were mentioned in Chapter Three. As a consequence of some situations described there and for other reasons discussed below, more than a fifth of active patients experienced problems at the point of discharge from either the Special Hospital or from NHS hospitals. These problems were spontaneously reported by supervisors during interviews and they arose for a similar proportion of both restricted and unrestricted patients, though since the former were more numerous, most incidents involved restricted patients.

There were 78 administrative problems, mostly concerning what supervisors regarded as insufficient preparation for patient discharge or inadequate information about patients at the point of discharge. Nearly half of all problems (37) arose because no or inadequate or unsatisfactory arrangements had been made for social and/or medical supervision. In some cases this was the result of misunderstandings about responsibility when supervision was shared; sometimes the current supervisor thought that it was the responsibility of the Home Office to arrange for changes of supervisor when a patient moved, or assumed that a letter sent to a colleague in the new area discharged formal responsibility for transferring supervision; sometimes a doctor did not wait for formal acceptance of supervision by a social supervisor but assumed notification to the head of the area agency had fulfilled the responsibility for arranging social supervision. Several agency members commented that the first they knew about supervision was an enquiry from the Home Office asking for a first report. Agencies also expressed concern over some cases where unrestricted patients were discharged to areas, sometimes where they had been well known, when it might have been an infringement of ethics for the Special Hospital to have advised local social agencies about their release. This was a particular problem for agencies supervising families of which the patient was a member and where his arrival (when it came to agency attention) was thought likely to exacerbate existing problems. Such circumstances account for some of 13 instances of problems which supervisors described as discharge to unsuitable environments. This might result from the inability of the Special Hospital to find an NHS place for a patient who no longer needed treatment in secure conditions, or a hostel place for a patient who needed no treatment at all and who was discharged by his Special Hospital doctor or by a tribunal directly into the community. Such patients, desperate for accommodation, might return to homes where their relatives found it difficult to deal with existing family commitments; or to relatives who provoked anxiety or irritation in patients. Some of the problems arose from discharge of patients to hostels catering for the mentally handicapped, or in some instances to hostels which were notoriously badly managed but were the only accommodation available.

In those 29 cases where arrangements for medical or social supervision were unsatisfactory, 14 patients involved (48 per cent) were readmitted to hospital and 11 of these admissions were serious. There was a statistically significant difference ($p < .05$) between involvement in grave psychiatric incidents by 32 per cent of patients involved in transfer problems and by 19 per cent for whom no such problems were reported.

Seven reports of inadequate information were made by social supervisors and three complaints about misleading information were made by medical supervisors. Social supervisors sometimes found themselves with Special Hospital patients as statutory clients after postdischarge reoffences but were unable to obtain from the Special Hospital information or advice to which they felt entitled. A few supervisors said they would not have accepted supervision if they had been in full possession of the facts. There are ethical problems about the exchange of information between social supervisors and doctors, see pages 41-42. It is also possible to give a truthful account of a patient's history which omits details a supervisor might wish to know; doctors endeavouring to arrange placements into the community may try to avoid handicapping patients by passing on circumstantial accounts of horrific offences which occurred many years earlier or of probable but unproven sexual overtones in admission offences of assault. More information might have alerted supervisors to the degree of risk for their client or patient but there were insufficient data to provide any conclusive evidence of relapse or reoffending in these circumstances.

Disclosure

Related to the problems concerning disclosure of sociomedical history were those discussed in Chapter Three, see pages 42-43, concerning the disclosure of patients' Special Hospital background. Scores were computed based on the percentage of disclosures of Special Hospital history made by patients in a number of circumstances when this might have been possible, see Appendix Table One. There were significant but weak associations between the three categories of disclosure scores and some incident measures:

Disclosure by:		x^2	df	sig.level	phi C.V
(i)	Psychiatric incidents (frequency)	18.14	4	<.001	.17
(ii)	Psychiatric incidents (weighted)	17.33	4	<.001	.16
(iii)	Criminal incidents (frequency)			not significant	
(iv)	Criminal incidents (weighted)			not significant	
(v)	All incidents (frequency)	17.54	4	<.002	.16
(vi)	All incidents (weighted)	16.80	4	<.002	.16

Discrimination by patient and supervisor about the circumstances in which disclosure should be made seems to be supported by the finding that disclosure in more than half but not all situations was associated with involvement in fewer incidents, a U-curve only apparent in the full tabulations, see for example Table 5.19 below.

Nearly half of those patients who disclosed in less than half (0-50 per cent) or in all possible (100 per cent) situations had been involved in psychiatric incidents. When all psychiatric incidents and weighted incidents are taken into account, patients with 100 per cent disclosure scores were involved in more frequent and more serious incidents. The association is probably reciprocal since it is hardly possible for a patient with frequent admissions to conceal a Special Hospital background; some were rather proud of the distinction or used their background in a manipulative way to impress or frighten fellow patients or others.

Table 5.19
Disclosure score by postdischarge psychiatric incidents (N330)

Disclosure Score		Psychiatric incidents None	One	Two +
0 - 50	[24%]	46 (57%)	24 (30%)	11 (14%)
51 - 99	[30%]	78 (80%)	12 (12%)	8 (8%)
100	[46%]	83 (55%)	40 (27%)	28 (19%)

x^2=18.14, df 4, p<.001; Cramer's V .17

113

There were no significant associations between disclosure scores and grid measures but when specific situations were examined there was a constant trend for lowered self esteem to be associated with disclosure and for those patients with high grid scores for integration and self percepts as independent to disclose in fewer situations.

The necessity to disclose (to employers by patients being closely supervised or to anyone knowing about hospital admissions) may be humiliating. The decision to disclose, but not indiscriminately, may be a sign of increasing selfconfidence and of successful reintegration.

There were also significant associations between the three categories of disclosure scores and both major diagnoses (p<.002; CV.21) and age (p<.004; CV.18). There was no association between disclosure scores and criminal incidents. Psychopaths apparently chose to disclose in a discriminating manner. Schizophrenics, more likely to be involved in psychiatric incidents, were more likely to disclose in all situations. Controlling diagnosis for age shows the pattern unchanged for young patients of either diagnostic category but a very slightly stronger association, as one might expect, for 100 per cent disclosure by older schizophrenics.

The preference of those administering Restriction Orders that patients should disclose their Special Hospital background was supported by evidence that disclosure, when made with some discrimination, was associated with less frequent involvement in incidents. Those secretive about their background and those who disclosed it in every possible situation were less likely to be successful and incident free than those who disclosed in more than half but not all possible situations. The insistence by some supervisors that patients should always disclose their backgrounds seems excessive and is likely to undermine self esteem. As time goes by it may be more important to think of reducing all possible sources of stigma for patients.

At risk situations

There was no association between incident or grid measures and the 'at risk' score, see Appendix One, which gave points to patients living with close relatives in situations likely to lead to relapse according to the authorities cited on page 88. This was not, as hypothesised at an early stage in analysis, because those who relapsed had been readmitted; there was no association between such scores and hospital admissions. All the evidence seems to indicate that relatives of Special Hospital patients should be assisted in looking after patients unless there is some profound indication to the contrary.

Summary

This chapter provided some evidence from the grid measure that rapport with an official supervisor assisted in reintegration of patients. There was no evidence that supervisors' criticism, which might indicate emotional involvement, adversely affected reintegration. In practice, the protection of patient self esteem may need to be considered. Excessive stress on disclosure of Special Hospital background in all circumstances seems likely to damage self esteem and a certain amount of discrimination in revealing patient history was associated with successful integration.

Later in the chapter, where incident measures were used in combination with other data, it was found that despite Restriction Orders, supervision was often nominal and patients might have lengthy supervision without much contact with supervisors or series of supervisors. This was often the case with patients who it has been argued are very likely to reoffend, young psychopaths who were also prone to be problem drinkers. Frequent and continuous care as well as hospital admissions were more likely to result from patient deviant behaviour than to forestall it.

Although being in employment was strongly associated with successful reintegration this finding may only have reflected the problems of finding and keeping employment by patients whose stay in the community was interrupted by spells in hospital or custody. Patients in employment did not have high self esteem perhaps because of the difficulty they had in obtaining satisfying work.

Hostels did not seem to be the most satisfactory accommodation for patients. Despite the fact that patients with low scores for integration were often living with close relatives, patients with hostel placements were more likely to be involved in incidents. The type of incident was related to their age and diagnosis. 'At risk' situations (those where patients were likely to have a high degree of contact with close relatives) which were shown to be detrimental for schizophrenics in other studies were not associated with relapse or recidivism for Special Hospital patients. This has implications for the involvement of families and provision of accommodation which are discussed in Chapter Seven.

Chapter Six compares some of the findings reported in the preceding chapters with some earlier studies of similar patients.

6 Comparison with two previous studies

Before discussing the implications of the findings from this study, it seems worth pausing to consider how and why these results differ from two other research reports published during the last few years. Black (1982) studied part of an earlier cohort of Broadmoor patients. Thornberry and Jacoby (1979) followed up a set of patients rather more similar to those studied by Norris.

Black's study

Black studied 128 Broadmoor patients who were absolutely or conditionally discharged during the years 1960 to 1965, 21 per cent of all separations, and he examined preadmission and postdischarge factors from official records using a follow up period of five years. The following comparisons were made with Black's detailed mimeographed report which was subsequently summarised and published (1982). Norris's 124 patients who were conditionally or absolutely discharged (see Table 1.1) amounted, like Black's, to 21 per cent of all patients leaving Broadmoor during the period researched. Findings for the two groups of patients were compared.

Differences between patients in the studies

There were differences between the two groups of patients in diagnosis and age, see Tables 6.1 and 6.3; both factors were associated with aspects of postdischarge careers for Norris's patients. The fact that Black's figures include all and not only the

116

predominant diagnoses (duplications account for the number and percentage in Black's data exceeding 128 and 100 per cent in Table 6.1) may affect comparisons but the differences recorded below are greater than any effects likely to be caused by modes of categorisation.

Table 6.1
Diagnoses (Black and Norris patients)

| | Black | | Norris | |
	N	% of 128	N	% of 124
Schizophrenics	33	[26%]	39	[32%]
Affective disorders	41	[32%]	3	[2%]
Psychopaths	54	[42%]	75	[61%]
Other	13	[15%]	7	[6%]

The percentage of psychopaths is lower for Black than for Norris possibly (according to Black, personal communication, November, 1982) because his patients were admitted prior to the cessation of capital punishment, a factor which he thinks may have influenced diagnoses. This argument is partially supported by the difference in admission offences between the two groups, see Table 6.2, which shows many more homicides and attempted homicides amongst Black's patients. The greater number of sexual offenders amongst Norris's patients cannot be explained in this way.

Table 6.2
Admission offences (Black and Norris patients)

| | Black | Norris |
	% of 128	% of 124
Homicide	48%	20%
Assaults/att.homicide	26%	36%
Arson (+ property, Black)	5%	16%
Acquisitive (+ property, Norris)	18%	7%
Sexual	3%	15%
Other	–	6%

Property offences (usually breaking windows or minor damage) only accounted for a handful of crimes amongst Norris patients, and it was thought reasonable to include these with acquisitive offences which are also associated with property. The fact that these offences were included with arson in Black's study is unlikely to affect the conclusions drawn below. The larger number of sexual crimes, offences associated with younger patients, is linked with the younger age range of Norris patients. There were also differences in lengths of stay in the Special Hospital, see Table 6.3 overleaf.

117

Table 6.3

Ages and lengths of Special Hospital stay (Black and Norris patients)

	Black	Norris
Mean age on admission in years	34.07	27.31
Range	16.5 - 65 years	15 - 58 years
Mean age at discharge	41.54	33.38
Range	21 - 71	19 - 63 years
Mean lengths of stay in years	7.48	6.12
Range	2mths - 40 years	4mths - 40 years

The categorisation of victims in the two studies differed. Black included victims 'known' to the offender with family victims and Norris did not. However, the major difference between the two studies was that Black's study included many more wives who were victims because of the far greater percentage of homicides, generally widowed as a result of their offence, among Black's patients. 33 per cent of Black's patients' victims were wives; only three per cent of Norris's patients' victims were wives.

The percentage of schizophrenics in both groups of patients was roughly similar but there were more psychopaths amongst Norris patients. Preadmission histories for both groups were associated, as Norris found, with postdischarge deviant behaviour. Previous hospital admissions were associated with schizophrenia and previous convictions with psychopathy. 48 per cent of Norris's patients and 50 per cent of Black's patients had previous hospital admissions, but 75 per cent of Norris's, compared to 60 per cent of Black's sample had previous convictions. Those of Black's patients who left in the later part of his study were (Black, personal communication, 1982) more like Norris's patients and he attributed changes in characteristics to a change in personnel responsible for recommending discharge in the early sixties.

The proportions of conditionally compared to absolutely discharged patients were similar in both groups of patients but (where information was available) 33 per cent of Black's compared to 46 per cent of Norris's patients were discharged to hostels rather than directly into the community, probably reflecting the growth in the small hostel movement in the intervening years (see Otto and Orford, 1978).

The educational and occupational backgrounds of the two samples were very similar if Black's 'armed forces' (a category too small for Norris to treat separately) are assumed to be largely 'unskilled'.

Norris specifically excluded patients who were not discharged for the first time during the period 1974 - 1981. The length of stay in the Special Hospital which Black attributed to patients is sometimes the brief period which immediately preceded a second or subsequent entry to the community (and age at discharge will also have been affected by the duplication of some patients who left twice during the period). If corrections were made for these factors Black's patients might have been even older and might have stayed even longer than Norris's.

Relapse

Norris patients had fewer postdischarge psychiatric admissions, see Table 6.4, a result to be expected since more of Norris patients were psychopathic and less likely to have such admissions. The 'psychiatric and Broadmoor' admissions include individuals who also appear in the previous two categories.

Table 6.4
Hospital events after discharge (Black and Norris patients)

	Black % of 125	Norris % of 124
Psychiatric admission	19%	12%
Broadmoor admission	19%	16%
Psychiatric and Broadmoor	9%	2%

It is also possible that there have been changes since 1965 in hospital management and policy affecting readmission. However, Norris patients had a longer time in the community during which they had opportunities to be readmitted. (It is possible that the exclusion by Norris of a fifth of separations which were not first time separations may also affect postdischarge comparisons but it is not thought that any great discrepancies result).

Recidivism

Norris patients also reoffended less, see Table 6.5, despite a longer follow up period (the modal period to interview was four years but 36 per cent were followed up for five or more years, some for as long as seven years).

Table 6.5
Offender events after discharge (Black and Norris patients)

	Black % of 125	Norris % of 124
Court appearances	40%	39%
Imprisonment	23%	13%
Further assaults committed	10%	6%

Lengths of time in the community

51 per cent of Black's and 66 per cent of Norris's patients remained in the community for the entire follow up period which, it has been pointed out already, was longer for the latter.

Time till first psychiatric recall was very similar for both groups of patients, the mean for Black's being 1 year 3 months and for Norris's slightly longer, 1 year 6 months. The reverse was the case for court appearances, where the mean was 1 year 4 months for Norris's patients, and 1 year 9 months for Black's patients. The time spent in the Special Hospital during periods of recall was much shorter for the Norris patients, a mean of 1 year 2 months (and brief 'visits' were not included) compared to Black's patients' mean of 2 years 1 month. Again the reverse is true for offender data, Norris's patients spending a mean of 3 years 2 months in prison and Black's patients a mean of 1 year 8 months, although the comparisons here may be affected by the longer Norris follow up period, and Norris patients returned to prison more quickly so that (because of the longer follow up for many Norris patients) mean lengths of stay would tend to be longer even if mean lengths of sentences were similar.

Common findings

Partly as a result of the different characteristics (and occasionally of differing categorisations) of the Norris and Black patients the significant associations found by Black between patient characteristics and postdischarge events were not often replicated.

Black found a significant association between type of victim and every kind of postdischarge variable. In Black's study there were 96 known victims; in Norris's there were only 25 (for this group of patients) and no significant associations between relationship of victim and postdischarge events. However, when the data for all 588 Norris patients and all offences was examined, three of the five associations with postdischarge events found by Black were also found by Norris and there was a suggestive but not significant relationship in a fourth instance. Sometimes the findings were rather predictable, however. Schizophrenics who were also homicides usually had wives as victims and homicides were found by Norris to be less likely to reoffend or relapse than any other type of patient; half of Black's patients were homicides and so a (negative) relationship between type of victim and relapse would be expected.

Further analysis of admission data for all Norris patients showed that all schizophrenics were significantly ($p < .002$; phi .24) more likely to have 'close relatives' as victims although their admission offence was more often an assault. Another predictable association found by Norris concerning victims was that sexual offences, usually by those diagnosed as psychopaths, were against 'other' victims, not wives, the finding being an artefact of the legal definition of rape. But only 12 per cent of psychopaths with a victim had a close relative as a victim compared to 41 per cent of schizophrenics. All significant associations found concerning victims and postdischarge events were attributable to the trouble free postdischarge careers of most homicides.

The association between preadmission history and postdischarge type of deviant behaviour reported by Norris was also found by Black. Some associations between psychopathy and reoffending were found by Black but none between schizophrenia and readmission, a finding also attributable to the predominance of homicides, generally diagnosed as schizophrenic.

The absence of the majority of schizophrenics, those who had been transferred to NHS hospitals, from Black's study means that all his findings must be very carefully qualified if used to predict postdischarge events. The small proportion of Norris patients discharged directly into the community had different characteristics from the majority of 'separated' patients. Black's omission of transferred patients accounts for most discrepancies between overall findings from the two studies. In particular, in the Norris study older patients were more likely to have postdischarge readmissions to hospitals than younger patients, a finding quite contrary to Black's because of the different characteristics of the patients studied.

Moreover, the further analysis undertaken by Norris showed that intervening and antecedent variables, such as supervision and diagnosis, influenced postdischarge careers.

Summary of comparison with Black's study

Both Black and Norris found some significant relationships between lengths of stay and postdischarge careers, but the dichotomy adopted by Black, it was argued in Chapter Four, conceals the effects of age which was responsible for less reoffending amongst patients whose stay in the Special Hospital was lengthy; otherwise trends were for short stays to be associated with less relapse and recidivism.

Some associations found by Black were also found by Norris, but differences in patients' characteristics and probable changes in policy affecting postdischarge events makes direct comparison difficult. However, taking into account the factors discussed, more of Norris's conditionally or absolutely discharged patients than Black's appear to have remained well and law abiding in the postdischarge period. This is despite the fact that they were younger and more frequently psychopathic than Black's patients and might therefore have been expected to be more at risk.

It did not seem that what appeared to have been a more recent policy of discharging patients who were younger, more at risk and who had stayed less time in Broadmoor resulted in any worse outcomes, rather the reverse.

Comparison with Thornberry and Jacoby's study.

Thornberry and Jacoby studied the postdischarge careers of 586 'Dixon' patients, who were transferred to other hospitals from Farview, an American institution which has some resemblance to Broadmoor. Their transfer was the result of a judicial decision in 1971 which found their detention in Farview unconstitutional. These were therefore not patients thought to be ready for discharge but about a third of the population of Farview and it was of some interest to see if this population, random as far as clinical decisions were concerned, differed greatly from the similar number of patients in the Norris study and if any differences affected their postdischarge careers. There were some problems in making comparisons, since Thornberry and Jacoby were only able to interview 17 per cent of their sample in the community and could only locate 44 per cent, and Norris's data for inpatients after discharge were less detailed than for patients who were 'active' and in the community; but it was possible to compare a considerable number of findings.

Mean age at admission was the same to one place of decimals (32.7 years) for both Dixon and Broadmoor patients. Dixon patients stayed in the hospital on average twice as long as Special Hospital patients (14 and 7 years respectively) and their average age at discharge was therefore also greater than Special Hospital patients' (47 years and 39 years respectively). Similar marital status was reported for Dixon and Broadmoor patients on admission (12 per cent and 15 per cent married) and similar proportions of each were brought up by someone other than a relative (9 per cent and 10 per cent respectively) although rather more Broadmoor patients were brought up by their natural parents, 76 per cent of those for whom information was available but 63 per cent of the whole sample, compared to 50 per cent of Dixon patients. The Pennsylvanian environment probably accounts for the much higher proportion of nonwhites amongst Dixon patients, 40 per cent compared to 12 per cent of Broadmoor patients, but the proportion of nonwhites is much greater than that in the general population in both instances. Broadmoor patients were rather better educated (six per cent having some further education compared to one per cent of Dixon patients) if some flexibility in interpreting American and British educational achievements allows comparisons to be made; but Broadmoor patients' education was also probably unrepresentative of the general Special Hospital population in this country (all Norris's patients were admitted to Broadmoor, although 34 spent part of their time in another Special Hospital before discharge, see pages 15-16 and 65). If farming, a major occupation in Pennsylvania, is included amongst the 'other than skilled' occupations, there were similar proportions of unskilled workers among Dixon and Broadmoor patients but fewer of the latter were unemployed on admission (two per cent Broadmoor compared to ten per cent Dixon). Fathers' occupations were very similar in both studies. On the whole, backgrounds were therefore similar.

Preadmission psychiatric histories differed, probably on account of differences between the USA and the UK in hospital admission policies and costs of hospitalisation as well as other environmental factors. Dixon patients had fewer prior hospital admissions (5 per cent had 'more than four' compared to 24 per cent 'more than four' amongst Special Hospital patients) and a smaller proportion (43 per cent) had any earlier admissions compared to Special Hospital patients (54 per cent). It is almost impossible to match USA and UK diagnostic categories but 347 Dixon compared to 363 Broadmoor patients were diagnosed as schizophrenic, suggesting a quite similar sample.

Preadmission criminal histories were also not too dissimilar, bearing in mind probable differences in law enforcement policy in the two environments. More Broadmoor patients (33 per cent) had no prior arrests (court appearances, in fact) than Dixon patients (19 per cent) but 31 per cent of Broadmoor patients with arrests had 'five or more' compared to 15 per cent of Dixon patients. Thornberry and Jacoby regard multiple arrests as an indication of recidivism and if this is true, then almost twice as many Broadmoor as Dixon patients were chronic offenders. The categories for violent offences were difficult to compare, since Thornberry and Jacoby, unlike Norris, include some violent sex offences in this category and exclude them from sexual offences. Using Thornberry and Jacoby's criteria, 41 per cent of preadmission offences for Dixon patients were violent and 13 per cent sexual; using Norris's criteria, 26 per cent of admission offences for Broadmoor patients were violent and 13 per cent sexual. If Thornberry and Jacoby's criteria were used almost all the Broadmoor patients' sexual offences would shift to the violent category, making a total of 39 per cent; and if Norris's criteria were used some of the Dixon patients' sexual offences would be included as 'other' or excluded - fornication and adultery are amongst those listed. The type of sexual offences of both sets of patients are therefore probably similar.

However, there were many more homicides amongst Norris's patients (27 per cent compared to 7 per cent of Dixon patients) and more violent crimes (75 per cent compared to 54 per cent of Dixon patients) though 12 per cent of Dixon patients were sexual offenders compared to 8 per cent of Broadmoor patients and Dixon patients had rather more 'other', that is usually less serious offences, 13 per cent compared to 8 per cent of Broadmoor patients. When allowance is made for differing categorisation, it seems likely that a rather higher proportion of Broadmoor patients had committed violent crimes.

There was therefore very little difference between Dixon patients and Broadmoor patients except that the former were randomly discharged and the latter selectively discharged; and it was probable that Broadmoor patients had more violent admission offences and were more often chronic offenders.

All Dixon patients were first transferred to other hospitals. The percentage of those who left these hospitals and entered the community is roughly equivalent to the 'active' Norris sample, 363 (62 per cent) Dixon patients and 330 (56 per cent) Special Hospital patients.

The numbers of residential moves of both groups of the discharged were similar and very similar percentages of Dixon and Special Hospital patients when first discharged went to live with parents (29 per cent and 28 per cent respectively); or with friends (3 per cent of both); or with other family (23 per cent and 19 per cent respectively). Fewer Special Hospital patients lived alone (10 per cent) at this stage than Dixon patients (27 per cent). Comparing last accommodation of Special Hospital patients and third accommodation of Dixon patients, more Special Hospital patients (39 per cent) were living with family members who were not their parents, mainly wives, than Dixon patients (18 per cent), although for both groups the percentage living with parents had halved. Equal proportions of Dixon and Special Hospital patients (32 per cent) were living alone in their latest accommodation. A considerable number (30 per cent) of Dixon patients were in institutions by this stage, a category not included in the Norris data, although if group homes are regarded as a similar category for the elderly or dependent there were only about 8 per cent so housed. Dixon patients were, of course, older at separation.

Special Hospital patients were more likely to be working (42 per cent excluding those in sheltered employment) than Dixon patients (28 per cent) despite the poor employment prospects in this country at the time of interview. Age was not associated with employment in either study.

Provision of aftercare for Special Hospital patients was often mandatory as the result of Restriction Orders and 82 per cent had a psychiatrist compared to 39 per cent of Dixon patients, although another 17 per cent of Dixon patients had a psychologist. The two professions are probably rather more interchangeable in America than in this country, where British restrictions require a medical doctor to be appointed. Also as a result of Restriction Orders, Special Hospital patients were almost twice as likely to have a social supervisor (90 per cent) compared to Dixon patients (50 per cent).

Because more of the chronic schizophrenic Dixon patients were still in hospital and Thornberry and Jacoby's research design gave them readier access to inpatients than Norris had, measures of adjustment for Dixon patients are probably biased towards the chronic schizophrenic section of their sample and not readily comparable with Norris's findings on integration. The instrument used by Thornberry and Jacoby (the Katz Adjustment Scale) was unsuitable for the Special Hospital study since it contained too many items which were thought likely to arouse anxiety in patients and it depended for validity on responses also being obtained from a relative or friend. (This appears to have created difficulties for Thornberry and Jacoby who seem only to have obtained such responses for a quarter of their sample in the community even when they extended the category to include hospital employees). Norris's grid measure was not designed for use with inpatients but the finding of Thornberry and Jacoby that length of stay in Farview did not affect adjustment of inpatients was replicated by Norris (using the grid measure) for all patients interviewed; Thornberry and Jacoby's finding, which they found difficult to explain, that longer Farview stays were associated with better psychological adjustment amongst those who had been readmitted to hospital may also be attributable to the decrease in deviant behaviour with age, as argued in the study reported here.

Thornberry and Jacoby were critical of the lack of official social support given to Dixon patients who entered the community. Special Hospital patients had more assistance in obtaining housing (43 per cent from family and friends, 44 per cent from official sources) than Dixon patients (34 per cent and 30 per cent respectively). The same proportion of Special Hospital patients received assistance from family and friends in finding employment as Dixon patients (11 per cent) but Special Hospital patients received twice as much official assistance, though still only 23 per cent did so. The level of employment amongst Dixon patients was regarded as unacceptably low by Thornberry and Jacoby at 28 per cent (although it is possible that Dixon patients had more physical disabilities than the Norris patients, see Thornberry and Jacoby, pp.137-140). Double the rate of official assistance may have contributed to the better employment record of Special Hospital patients although a very substantial percentage obtained their own employment. Medication is not discussed in the Thornberry and Jacoby study and this may also affect ability to work.

A few more (49) Dixon patients received prison sentences after discharge than Special Hospital patients (42), the latter during a much longer follow up period, sometimes seven or eight years compared to at most four years for Dixon patients. Many more Dixon patients were formally committed to hospital (41 compared to 13 readmitted to either the Special Hospital or an NHS hospital) following a court appearance in connection with an offence. The rate of court appearances (or arrests) for both Special Hospital and Dixon patients was about the same, even when controlled for age. Because of the longer follow up period for Special Hospital patients and their comparative youth, it might be anticipated that they would appear in court more often than Dixon patients. The similar rate of recidivism suggests that Special Hospital patients' behaviour was less deviant than would be expected, all other things being equal.

Summary of comparison with Thornberry and Jacoby's study

Dixon patients were a random sample of Farview patients transferred out of a secure hospital as a result of a judicial decision. Dixon patients and Special Hospital patients had similar characteristics apart from the higher age at discharge of Dixon patients compared to Special Hospital patients, due to average stays in Farview of about twice the length of stays in Broadmoor; and there were probably more violent crimes amongst Special Hospital patients' admission offences. Postdischarge careers of Special Hospital patients for employment, accommodation, and recidivism were better than those of the Dixon patients. This may have been the result of some aspects of supervision discussed in Chapter Seven. In that chapter some suggestions are made, based on the findings from the Special Hospital study, concerning those aspects of aftercare which seemed to have had most effect upon patients' careers.

7 Discussion and recommendations

Introduction to review of the study

Respondents and sponsors occasionally expressed the hope that findings would predict postdischarge careers with an accuracy which would reduce problems for all those responsible for recommending discharge. Predictions of that kind can only sum probabilities and might therefore be misleading in any individual case. It has also to be remembered that the findings reported here concern only discharged patients and it would require a different kind of study to demonstrate that, for example, a three year stay in a Special Hospital would suffice for all patients. Moreover it has been argued throughout this book that factors other than patient characteristics influenced postdischarge careers.

There is almost limitless opportunity to pursue secondary analysis of the data collected; for example, further analysis which will attempt to establish some kind of hierarchical order of importance amongst factors is now proposed. However, findings from studies of this kind are frequently reported to be out of date by the time all desirable analysis has been completed and some such objections have already been voiced, as will be seen below, about this report. In these circumstances it seems preferable to publish findings to date without delay and in a form which is comprehensible to workers in this field, whilst acknowledging that there are an infinite variety of methodological refinements and additional work needing to be undertaken. Meanwhile any patient or a person interested in his welfare can see that some characteristics make certain eventualities more likely than others, but variations in aftercare for which the patient is not responsible may be associated with different outcomes. A few of the areas where intervention by others affects patient careers are reviewed later in this chapter, followed by some suggestions which may guide provision of more positive and helpful assistance to patients. It should be remembered that these findings are not applicable to women or to men other than those of normal intelligence discharged from the Special Hospitals.

It would be graceless to omit to mention the contribution which patients made to this study, although acknowledgements are also made elsewhere. Patient interviews gave rise to some concern over ethics as well as much curiosity amongst other respondents and collaborators and some comment seems appropriate before summarising findings. Considerable efforts were made to avoid any suggestion that patient cooperation was obtained under duress, see Chapter Two, and each patient was given a further opportunity to refuse to cooperate in the privacy of the interview setting. The lower response rate amongst recently discharged patients, see page 9, suggests that patients were not inhibited from refusing to cooperate. Those interviewed were, with rare exceptions, welcoming and sometimes very anxious to talk. Some were lonely and the interview was welcome for that reason. To avoid arousing anxiety, interviewers never raised issues concerning admission offences or stays in the Special Hospital but patients often volunteered information although the use of the grid form did not encourage them to do so. One or two found recollections distressing but were determined to pursue the topic, perhaps finding relief in talking about a part of their life which they rarely discussed with others.

Doctors' suggestions that interviewers might report any signs of relapse were not acceptable on ethical grounds and interviewers were not in any case qualified to identify such signs. (Dishevelment and bizarre responses, for example, suggested as possible indicators of patients' relapse, were occasionally recorded by interviewers as characterising other respondents). Although some patients' postdischarge careers were eventful, few gave interviewers cause for alarm. One behaved in an unnerving manner (and the social supervisor said, too late to be helpful, that the patient was frightening) but nothing untoward occurred. One or two had mannerisms or obsessional topics of conversation which were bizarre but apparently harmless. One obtained an interviewer's telephone number and made a nuisance of himself for a brief period. The majority of patients were pleasant and cooperative and interviewers recorded extremely favourable impressions of some patients. Of course, these may have been only the most well and the most amenable patients. Some were unlikeable and cantankerous like any other members of the public occasionally encountered in similar field work and the low grid scores of some patients suggested that not all were in perfect psychological health.

Many had put aside their past history, survived lengthy stays in hospital without becoming institutionalised and overcome stigma and financial and other problems in a wholly admirable manner. It is regretted that confidentiality prevents more detailed descriptions of the way in which some patients had successfully battled against adversity.

One general conclusion which could be drawn from the findings was reassuring. The majority of patients in the community, despite the circumstances leading to their admission, were managing well. They were less likely to be readmitted to hospital or to reoffend than they had been before admission, and if their behaviour was deviant they were more likely to be involved in less serious reoffences and informal admissions than in more serious incidents, see page 49. Rather less than one in ten of all patients was likely to be involved in an assaultive or sexual offence or arson. Two of the most serious postdischarge offences were committed by patients whilst in other secure custodial institutions but the percentage of those in the community who reoffended was higher than the percentage for all patients, see page 45. Opportunities for offending were perhaps greater in the community and financial problems may have motivated some offences although NHS hospital patients could and did reoffend (and 'seriously relapse' by committing or attempting suicide or behaving in a way which led to recall to the Special Hospital). Less serious deviant behaviour of patients in hospital seems much less likely to be defined as criminal activity but more serious deviant behaviour is considered to be reliably recorded for NHS inpatients in this study.

Supervisors (and patients) can consult Chapter Four for information on the likelihood of further incidents for a patient with or without various kinds of preadmission history, and can also take into account the likely effects of his admission offence, diagnosis (bearing in mind the possibility that admission diagnosis might occasionally be misleading), drinking habits and age at discharge. If the patient is black or brown his mannerisms may disconcert the helping services and he may have trouble with the police but he is likely to be at least as well behaved and probably rather better integrated than a white patient with similar characteristics.

Those patients whose admission offences caused most anxiety to their supervisors, the homicides, were least likely to relapse or reoffend. Problem drinkers were those most at risk of reoffending although they also had characteristics which meant that they were less closely supervised. Those with admission offences of assault, who were often psychopathic, younger and problem drinkers, were for all these reasons rather more liable to reoffend than other patients (55 per cent did so) and they were more numerous than other types of offender. Sexual offenders who reoffended were very likely to commit a similar crime: however, only 33 of 48 sexual offenders who were 'separated' became 'active' and although more than a third of these active patients reoffended, the total number was small.

Diagnosis, supervisory assistance and some other environmental factors discussed below were influential factors associated with patient careers in the community. Reconsideration of these factors might improve the efficiency of the helping professions and others concerned with patient welfare in preventing or reducing relapse and recidivism and might also make life less difficult for patients after discharge.

Diagnosis

Admission diagnosis, regardless of patients' state of health at discharge, influenced the ways in which they entered the community and attitudes of people in the community, including official supervisors and the police.

Doctors acknowledged the difficulty of making diagnoses at the time of admission and some demurred at the term being used at all for their intervention at this stage, but it is necessary for a diagnosis to be agreed by two doctors to fulfil the legal requirements before a patient can be admitted to the Special Hospital. All the postdischarge consequences of admission diagnoses could not have been foreseen and some diagnoses were certainly made rather arbitrarily, see for example the quotation on page 19. Amongst a few transcripts of court proceedings where admission was agreed to be the best disposal for an offender some showed that a doctor who at first expressed doubts about a precise diagnosis might defer to his colleague's opinion, or both might compromise by agreeing that a patient showed symptoms of both psychopathy or personality disorder and schizophrenia, in order to meet the requirements of the Mental Health Acts that one or the other condition was present.

Social histories seem to have been extremely influential when diagnoses were being formulated, and it was suggested in Chapter Three that some young patients diagnosed as psychopathic, with consequences which have been discussed, might have been diagnosed as schizophrenic had they spent more time in the community before admission to the Special Hospital. It may be that doctors tend, consciously or not, to make some diagnosis other than schizophrenia when alternatives present themselves for young patients with no previous hospital admissions. Doctors will be aware of practical disadvantages for patients of a diagnosis of schizophrenia, although it is probable that for patients admitted to a Special Hospital the stigma of their stay in the institution may create similar problems. (Patients may not be able to enter certain employments, or adopt a child, or move to some other countries). It is more likely that doctors are uneasy about longterm effects on young patients of the medication most frequently prescribed for schizophrenics. The number of patients with postdischarge careers atypical for their diagnoses, for example psychopaths taking major tranquillisers for many years or being readmitted to hospital on a number of occasions after discharge, and the many nonwhite 'active' schizophrenics, suggest some possibility of misdiagnoses.

Whatever the circumstances of its formulation, the diagnosis for which the patient was formally admitted would be entered on his case history as either mental illness, usually schizophrenia, or psychopathy or personality disorder. When the patient was discharged as symptom free any later changes of opinion after observation would not alter the record of his Special Hospital admission diagnosis, which continued to figure prominently in his case notes. The evidence in this study suggests that this influenced his career.

Discharged patients who had a diagnosis of psychopathy or personality disorder were less sympathetically regarded than schizophrenics although they were often poorly integrated and needed rehabilitatory assistance. It would be preferable to defer a firm clinical diagnosis until the patient had been admitted for observation and testing. Until then, a descriptive assessment and a diagnosis of unspecified mental disorder might be adopted and records completed in a manner which met the conditions of the Mental Health Acts but which avoided premature but definitive labelling.

Lengths of stay in hospitals

It did not seem to be the case, as doctors thought, that the Home Secretary, exercising the powers invested in him by virtue of the Mental Health Acts, was primarily responsible for determining the lengths of time patients stayed in hospital, see page 23. Patients subject to Restriction Orders did not stay longer than the unrestricted although it is possible, but rather unlikely in view of the general trend, that those 25 per cent of patients with admission offences of homicide and who were almost always restricted are exceptions. There is insufficient evidence to support or refute the argument for these offenders but it is notable that sexual offenders, like those with admission offences of homicide, had long stays in the Special Hospital; 30 per cent of sexual offenders were not restricted and there was no significant difference in lengths of stay between the restricted and unrestricted. The assaultive had average lengths of stay, 30 per cent were not restricted, and there was no significant difference between lengths of stay for the restricted or unrestricted.

Evidence in Chapter Four showed that long stays in the Special Hospital were not associated with better outcomes for patients, rather the reverse, and it was argued that in these circumstances long stays may be primarily custodial. Special Hospital doctors, responsible for a great many discharges, are perhaps on that account more likely to stress their responsibility to the public than their colleagues in the community who are often concerned with the individual welfare of one or two patients who have previously been cleared for discharge from the Special Hospital by staff there.

Lengths of stays in NHS hospitals were much shorter than Special Hospital doctors anticipated during the period researched, when 'stability in an institution' was stated to be the Special Hospital aim for the majority of transferred patients. Two-thirds of patients transferred to NHS hospitals were in the community at the date of latest information and almost three-quarters had spent some time in the community. Of these more than 10 per cent left the transfer hospital within three months, 22 per cent within six months, 50 per cent within a year and 80 per cent within two years.

To NHS doctors supervising patients in hospitals where the average stay was about three weeks (apart from some chronically ill patients who were according to doctors quite different from the majority of discharged Special Hospital patients) these stays seemed extremely long. Special Hospital doctors may regard them as astonishingly short. It seemed that the advice of doctors in Special Hospitals and in NHS hospitals (although the two sets of doctors differed about what constituted an appropriate length of stay) had generally been accepted by the Home Secretary; those instances where it was not accepted or delays occurred were insufficiently frequent to alter the general patterns of lengths of stay advocated by the medical profession in either situation. NHS doctors could more often have applied for approval to exercise their discretion in giving leave or terminating regular contact with outpatients still subject to Restriction Orders. There were relatively few instances where such approval was withheld compared to the number of instances where doctors who said their patient was not ill had not taken this initiative. The fact that some doctors were not prepared to lapse supervision unless the Home Secretary terminated the Order might be regarded by the Home Office as an indication of some lack of confidence in the doctors' expressed views that supervision was unnecessary. However, some doctors gave as a reason for wishing to terminate supervision, that treatment was unavailing, and this will be discussed later.

Doctors played a more influential part than had been anticipated in determining, though sometimes by default, lengths of patients' stays in hospital, lengths of supervision and (by the diagnosis made at admission) the pathways into the community which facilitated or denied patients access to rehabilitation in hospital.

The role of the family

In this project findings about the role of close relatives were inconsistent with those of authorities such as Leff, or indeed of theorists like Laing and Cooper, who regarded the family as a contributory factor in relapse. Any explanation can only be speculative but it is probable that Special Hospital patients were much less ill than patients studied by the authorities cited. Special Hospital patients had often been waiting to leave for some time after their discharge had been approved (see Dell, 1980) and they seemed to be discriminating in their choice of family helper. No patient named a critical mother as a first choice helper, for example, a choice which the authorities cited on pages 88 and 89 might have predicted to be associated with relapse.

The patient's choice of helper was not always approved by the Special Hospital consultants whose views on family interest were reported on pages 27 and 28. Divorce generally precluded the return to their wives of patients with morbid jealousy (in two cases, incidentally, the exwife married the man who was the focus of the jealousy) but problems of accommodation did result in the return of some matricides, patricides, fratricides and infanticides to their families, if not at discharge then quite soon afterwards. Only one such case in the study was totally unsuccessful, leading to a well publicised relapse, though the disorganised state of some of these families worried supervisors. No family therapy or predischarge or postdischarge programmes designed to lessen the strain for these patients and their families were reported by respondents or recorded in case histories.

Contrary to expectations, in the present study schizophrenics were not less well integrated than other patients whose first choice helpers were close relatives, nor did degree of contact affect the findings. All patients whose first choice helpers were close relatives were significantly more likely to have low scores for integration than those choosing other unofficial helpers but a higher percentage (not significantly higher) of psychopaths than schizophrenics choosing close relatives as helpers had low scores for integration. The explanation for the predominance of low scores amongst all patients whose helpers were close relatives seemed to be that in the long run only their families were prepared to offer support to poorly integrated patients. For psychopaths there was less possibility of admission to hospital and they were also likely to receive the least continuous and most infrequent supervision. The problems which this group presented were of a kind which hospitals and social supervisors found difficult: one doctor explained that a patient had been discharged from hospital because no one there could influence or control his behaviour; his mother was able to do so.

Close relatives who looked after patients were unlikely to have had much contact with doctors in the Special Hospitals, although prospective wives may have been called in for a formal warning or to ensure that the patient had disclosed his background. The only predischarge contact some families received was a visit from an

133

otherwise uninvolved social worker in the course of formal enquiries which precede discharge. For further details of patient and social work contacts with relatives see Scott (1979) and Vaughan (1980).

Special Hospital staff report that this situation has now changed. It will be necessary to examine the arrangements made for a representative sample of recent discharges to demonstrate that this is in fact the case and a request for funding for this work has been made. The social work department at Broadmoor is known to have grown very rapidly during recent years but since some patients when completing separation grids had to give a surrogate for a social worker because they did not know one, the procedures were not always ideal as late as 1981. The Department of Health and Social Security also consider that social workers in the community are now more stable in post and better qualified to deal with forensic patients than the evidence in this report suggests.

Families were found to be a considerable source of support to patients, often accommodating them, frequently assisting them to find their first employment and reintroducing them to a circle of friends and acquaintances. (Some recent studies suggest that these findings apply to other psychiatric patients, see Collis and Ekdawi, 1982; and Collis and Ekdawi, 1983). Since, whatever the disadvantages of family life for a patient may be, only families were prepared to accept responsibility for many Special Hospital patients, family members should perhaps be given more thoughtful consideration by those responsible for supervision and it will be suggested later in this chapter that they should be included in plans for discharge from both Special Hospitals and NHS hospitals.

Supervision

There were two main influences upon supervision. The first was the policy of the Special Hospital during the period researched: 'Our aim is not rehabilitation but danger free resettlement'. (In 1984 this aim was stated to have changed and rehabilitation from the time of admission was said to be current policy, although it was acknowledged that changes in Special Hospital policy take time to implement). The second resulted from restrictions imposed under Orders made at the time of admission to the Special Hospital. Conditions of discharge were interpreted by many supervisors as defining for them a watchdog role concerned more with the welfare of the public than that of the patient. Special Hospital doctors and the Home Office, understandably, had public welfare firmly in mind and Special Hospital doctors also argued that it was in the general interest of all patients that the public should have no cause for alarm as a result of the behaviour of any discharged patients. There seemed, however, to be some conflict between Home Office concern for public safety and NHS doctors' concern for the individual patient.

However, medical and social supervisions in the community appeared to respond to rather than shape patients' behaviour. There were few constructive programmes for rehabilitation which attempted to reduce the possibility of recidivism or relapse other than by endeavours to ensure, when this was thought appropriate, that medication continued. A few hospitals which had rehabilitation programmes and continued to supervise patients in the community catered almost exclusively for 'burned out' schizophrenics, a category which accounted for perhaps nine per cent of Special Hospital patients; this situation was stated by the Department of Health and Social Security to have changed by 1984. Many medical and social supervisors stated that they did not understand their role in supervision, that the patient did not benefit, and that they and or the patient resented it. Better integrated patients were significantly more likely to resent supervision. Reoffence, rather than relapse, in these circumstances was almost a relief, since the man would then be dealt with by the penal system and worrisome and unsatisfactory supervision of him as a 'patient' would cease. Some extraordinarily callous remarks in a similar vein were recorded concerning the suicides of a few patients, though some supervisors were grieved at what they saw as a failure of their own professional support or of the support system as a whole.

A formula often adopted when a patient engaged in deviant behaviour and supervisory services were at a loss to know how else to proceed was that 'treatment had been unavailing and the law should take its course'. The effect was that behaviour, which had previously been regarded as symptomatic of illness or disorder and for which therefore the patient was not held responsible, even if he thought he should be, was redefined as criminal. The patient now became responsible for behaviour which had justified his incarceration for years for treatment. If the behaviour had ever been symptomatic of mental disorder then failure to change it resulted from a current lack of knowledge comparable to that preventing cure or control of cancer. These cases included some where patients committed offences which were not serious but which worried supervisors because of patients' previous history. The statement that treatment had been unavailing effectively precluded readmission to any hospital, including the Special Hospital, even when patients wished to return. The alternative was a series of prison sentences although supervisors often thought that the patients were not responsible for their behaviour. Some kind of benign custodial provision for people whose behaviour can neither be tolerated nor controlled, by themselves, the forces of law and order or the medical profession, might meet the needs of these patients.

'Dixon' patients did rather worse in the community than Special Hospital patients in this study, see Chapter Six. Thornberry and Jacoby (1979) were extremely critical of the lack of supervision and aftercare for Dixon patients. The system of mandatory supervision for 80 per cent of the sample in the present study may be responsible for some of the better outcomes for Special Hospital patients. The evidence presented in Chapter Five about the rudimentary supervision received by some of them does not suggest that this is a sufficient explanation. Dixon patients differed mainly from Special Hospital patients in having much longer stays in hospital. If patients deteriorate during lengthy stays in secure hospitals that would explain much of the difference between Dixon and Special Hospital patients' postdischarge careers.

Restriction Orders did ensure that the majority of patients had supervision. Although no differences in integration were found between the restricted and unrestricted, the higher rate of relapse and recidivism amongst those for whom transfer arrangements had broken down, see pages 111-112, seems to indicate that mandatory supervision is beneficial at the point of discharge or reentry to the community from the Special or NHS hospital or other institution. Restriction Orders do not, however, ensure (and are not intended to ensure) that supervision is continuous, frequent, or suitably devised for the kind of adjustment to the community which might prevent relapse or recidivism. Indeed, since the majority of supervisors had very limited experience of such patients or clients and there are great differences between various kinds of patients discharged from the Special Hospitals, it would be difficult for any isolated supervisor to formulate any clear plan or to know whether this was realistic, aimed too low or was too ambitious. The only universally common feature of supervision was the negative one anticipating relapse or recidivism, an attitude liable to become a self-fulfilling prophecy. The notions that if a patient is not offending or relapsing he must be 'doing well', or 'no news is good news', were not supported by evidence of very low scores for integration amongst some patients who were assessed as doing well by their supervisors. Moreover, such a negative attitude to a patient's return to the community can do little to increase self esteem, a self percept associated with socially acceptable behaviour.

Frequent changes of social supervision, it was argued, hindered establishment of the rapport associated with patient integration. Although patients often named social supervisors as helpers, these supervisors did not often rank highly amongst people of importance to the patient. Some of the few who were important to the patient were past supervisors whose supervision had been disrupted.

Collaborative exercises have in the past been found to be problematic (DHSS, 1978) and in this study collaborative supervision was common although team members did not always meet. A patient might receive visits from a community nurse or visit his family doctor for medication, might see his psychiatrist occasionally and his social worker or probation officer frequently. The psychiatrist or social supervisor might consult the Home Office or a Special Hospital doctor occasionally. The consequence was that there were quite often misunderstandings about how responsibility for the patient was shared, differences of opinion about disclosure, lack of communication of information and confusion about whether or not a patient was taking medication. So long as only one person in this team constantly and frequently saw the patient, or no one saw him often, these differences of opinion did not come to light. However, although social supervisors saw patients frequently they also changed quite often and shifts in perspective must sometimes have been bewildering for patients; some misunderstandings might have had serious consequences if a crisis occurred. Recommendations made for an agreed programme of rehabilitation might ensure a measure of agreement between the various persons involved and facilitate smoother handovers where changes of supervisor cannot be avoided.

Rehabilitation

Despite long stays in the Special Hospital and some quite lengthy stays in NHS hospitals after discharge, relatively few patients had received training in social or employment skills. Courses available for employment training were not highly regarded by patients and few used skills acquired during training. There were a number of requests by patients for more structured training for themselves and their supervisors in the necessary rehabilitatory skills, and supervisors who recognised these needs also said that they would like the opportunity to have training in methods of rehabilitation.

There is only one rehabilitation unit which caters specifically for Special Hospital patients. Patients there were almost all referred by Rampton Special Hospital and Moss Side and the unit was only briefly involved with any patient in this study. The evidence available concerning the number of discharges from Rampton and the number accepted by this unit suggests that selection is quite stringent; staff at the unit argue that selectivity occurs at the referral stage. For whatever reason, the unit was often under occupied. Its major disadvantage as a rehabilitation unit for Special Hospital patients in this study is that it only caters for men and is therefore unable to deal with the problems patients found in relating to women, see pages 30 and 33. It might be thought to be relatively inaccessible but it does claim to be able to establish the kind of predischarge links advocated below for patients and members of their proposed support networks in the community.

Recommendations

Recommendations were made early in 1983 to the Department of Health and Social Security. In March, 1984 the Department responded with some criticisms of methodology which were answered at a subsequent meeting to the apparent satisfaction of the academics present. Some further work is in hand or awaiting funding where further analysis would be valuable, mostly in connection with the establishment of relative importance of factors but also including a follow up to test prediction of incidents by the grid measure and a check, not strictly necessary on theoretical grounds but undertaken to rebut possible criticism, on any differences between grids completed by schizophrenics and other patients.

Recommendations were also discussed in 1984. Rewording and reordering to meet objections have not yet been agreed, but the substance of the recommendations with one exception has not been changed. The major objections raised were that events had overtaken recommendations. This was stated to be the case, for example, in connection with proposed rehabilitation programmes in Broadmoor and in other hospitals; with the incorporation of family members in proposed planning for discharge; and with the proposed encouragement of throughcare of Special Hospital patients by social supervisors in the community. This will be welcome news to some respondents and a proposed study to test one of these claims has already been mentioned. Recommendations are nevertheless reported in some detail since policy changes take time to implement, and research findings showed that expectations were not always fulfilled in practice. Some recommendations, for example that concerning regional groups, were regarded by some as a counsel of perfection and unworkable but were said by others to be coming into partial operation in some regions. Some recommendations, it was objected, were the result of the writer's preconceptions rather than being based on evidence from the report. Revisions were made to distinguish evidence from hard or soft data, and recommendations based on the latter were redefined as suggestions. One peripheral recommendation concerning government policy related to alcohol was withdrawn since it had never been claimed that it was supported by evidence from this study.

Generally, it was recommended that findings should be publicised concerning, for example, the social consequences for patients of firm diagnoses formulated at the time of admission. It was suggested that it would be preferable to defer such diagnoses whenever possible until they could be grounded in clinical and psychological testing and observation. It was thought that problem drinkers should be recognised to be at risk (the Department's social work representative expressed some anxiety lest this should then become a self-fufilling prophecy). It should also be made known that patients who had committed homicide were least likely to relapse or reoffend; and that supervisors and others caring for patients who have ceased medication should take comfort from the fact that this was not a factor associated with relapse in this study.

Some recommendations mainly concerned the Home Office, for example that they might reconsider their decision made on grounds of economy to cease acknowledging receipt of quarterly reports from supervisors, since one of the major dissatisfactions expressed by supervisors concerned the 'faceless bureaucracy' and the feeling that they sent reports into a void. Independent reports from social and medical supervisors are probably a better safeguard against misunderstandings over shared responsibility than arrangements, not uncommon, where one supervisor passes on to the Home Office the comments of the other. It might be helpful to provide each new supervisor, including registrars or locums where these submit reports on behalf of formally appointed supervisors, with the usual instructions given to first appointed supervisors and to remind first and subsequent social and medical supervisors of the desirability of exchanging information, copies of reports, etc. Although Restriction Orders were unpopular their retention might ensure mandatory supervision of most patients at important stages of transition, but it was suggested that an Order should be withdrawn when a programme of planned rehabilitation had been successfully concluded, thus giving supervisors and patient a goal and an incentive to achieve it.

Some recommendations and suggestions concerned rehabilitation. Since discharged patients did not appear to have benefited from periods of treatment longer than three years in the Special Hospital, and because public attitudes led to their detention for long periods after treatment ceased or behaviour stabilised, more constructive use of this time was suggested. This might in turn result in a reduction of subsequent time under restrictions in the community. Commencing rehabilitation in Broadmoor, as recommended, might offset any unease which psychiatrists and other staff may feel about their role in the detention of patients for long periods either after discharge has been recommended or after treatment has ceased to be effective. If the effect of this unease was refusal by the Special Hospital to accommodate homicides for long periods this might result in the committal of all homicides to prison although some might have benefited from treatment. The same might happen to sexual offenders for whom prison is generally thought an undesirable placement. The more humane approach might be to adopt a rehabilitatory programme of treatment designed to prevent deterioration for these and other longstay patients. (See page 134 for a statement concerning current policy).

Planned rehabilitation programmes, it was suggested, should be agreed with all concerned, not least the patient, prior to discharge. Especially for patients not subject to restrictions such programmes should be implemented during a period of leave before discharge is confirmed. For all patients the programme should begin before discharge or leave begins; the long wait for either Home Office approval or a hospital or hostel place should be constructively used so that the period when a patient might otherwise deteriorate is used for purposes which may be seen to shorten the time spent under restrictions after discharge. It was suggested to Broadmoor staff that they might consider obtaining funds or setting up a voluntary housing association to collect and administer funds which would provide accommodation, not necessarily in hostels, for patients moving into the community. Some NHS hospitals have already adopted this strategy, more could do so.

Greater consideration, it was suggested, should be given to the role of the family, especially parents, in the return to the community of patients discharged from both the Special Hospital and NHS hospitals. If the patient agrees, a family member or other unofficial helper should be encouraged to participate in decisions about discharge and predischarge preparations.

It was proposed that multidisciplinary liaison groups should be formed in each health area to review the implementation of rehabilitation programmes. Members might include Special Hospital staff or others responsible for designing rehabilitation programmes; representatives of the groups of hospitals and agencies most often concerned with the supervision of patients, not overlooking family doctors and community nurses; and possibly a representative of the Home Office, a representative of patients' families, and a representative of patients. Regular group meetings might go some way to meeting supervisors' (especially doctors') requests for more face-to-face discussion of individual patient progress; and it would facilitate the combination of experience, knowledge and attitudes currently available either in the Special Hospital or sparsely distributed in the community.

It would, it was suggested, benefit patients and staff if there was more collaboration between the Special Hospital and NHS hospitals. NHS nursing staff were not usually interviewed unless they were formally supervising patients but it was apparent that some were more important to patients in the community than their formally appointed supervisors, knew more about them and saw them more often if the patient received medication. However, some patients supervised by nurses had had little help with welfare benefits or in obtaining employment and achieving independence. More use could be made of community nurses in rehabilitation if they could, for example, help with patients' social security benefits and if they were trained in or advised about rehabilitation designed to raise patients' self esteem. Special Hospital nurses have had a bad press but at least one patient was extremely friendly with a Broadmoor nurse who might well have been his chosen social supervisor, given suitable training. If this facilitated cooperation in rehabilitation outside the Special Hospital it would add a new dimension to nursing there which might assist recruitment to an otherwise rather isolated speciality; and it might improve the public image of Special Hospital nursing staff. In addition it might modify the differences in relationship between patients and Special Hospital staff and patients and NHS hospital staff which were recorded in 'soft data' and seemed undesirable. Social workers in the Special Hospital might also find it rewarding to be able to participate in such a scheme. It was surprising to find that none of the Broadmoor social work staff, unlike those in some other Special Hospitals, took part in formal supervision of male patients including those supervised by doctors in the Special Hospital and living nearby, although this situation is reported to have changed since research ended. Psychologists in the Special Hospitals and NHS hospitals will certainly wish to contribute to the design and implementation of any programme for rehabilitation.

Patients who 'perceived similarity' with their chief official helper, indicating rapport and shared attitudes, achieved higher scores for integration. It was recommended that efforts should be made to ensure frequency and continuity of supervision by identifying the likely chief official helper, whether this be a doctor or a social supervisor, before the patient leaves the Special Hospital and promoting opportunities for the establishment of rapport. It would be better to identify incompatibility and to try another helper at this stage than after discharge. For patients without families a panel of discharged patients willing to be of unofficial assistance might be compiled. Patients who were extremely successful in the community reported that they had been discouraged from returning to talk to patients awaiting discharge; and visits by discharged patients to friends they have made in the Special Hospital have been discouraged, according to some reports, to avoid embarrassment to nursing staff, a situation which did not seem to occur in NHS hospitals. Sometimes visits were thought likely to upset either the visitor or the inpatient, but disturbing interaction might be better worked through under supervision than later when patients try to revive relationships after both have left the Hospital. Several patients mentioned that they would welcome an invitation to be of assistance. If this cannot be organised with the help of the Special Hospital some self help association facilitating contact between those patients well established in the community and those newly discharged might be fostered by supervisors in the community. There are, understandably, some patients who never wish to be reminded of their experiences or meet another patient and they would certainly not wish to help or be helped in this way; some would want to exercise some choice about whom they met; and there may be some volunteers whose assistance would be universally unwelcome. Self help groups accustomed to dealing with problems of this kind would not find them insurmountable.

In any case the chief helper should be incorporated in the team planning the rehabilitation programme. Sometimes a preadmission supervisor wished to keep in touch with a patient throughout his stay, and in view of the effects of rapport it was recommended that this should be encouraged. Some Special Hospital doctors objected to this practice on the grounds that these supervisors carry burdens of guilt which retard patient recovery if the relationship is maintained. It would seem preferable for such problems to be worked through and openly resolved if supervisors are to gain from experience and agencies are to profit and learn from situations which must recur from time to time in such collaborative enterprises. The alternative apparently leaves a conscientious and potentially useful colleague with unresolved problems of some magnitude and patients interpreted these unexplained lapses in throughcare as abandonment. A representative from the Hospital in 1984 stated that it had long adopted a policy of throughcare of the kind recommended.

It was recommended that supervisors (including social supervisors) be reminded from time to time of their ability to exercise discretion concerning recommendations to the Home Office that Orders should be terminated, leave arranged, etc. and they should be aware that this may take time. 'The bureaucratic mind needs to be prepared for action', said one supervisor whose reports over a period were carefully worded to demonstrate patient progress. NHS doctors also need to be reminded that accommodation and employment need not be lost to patients awaiting approval for discharge if leave and rehabilitatory programmes are already planned and agreed in anticipation of such opportunities. Evidence suggests that supervisors need to be reminded that they may exercise discretion concerning selective disclosure of Special Hospital background and that neither total secrecy nor total disclosure was associated with desirable outcomes.

Findings concerning medication and the tendency of other authorities to interpret behaviour differently for patients having medical treatment should be considered by doctors supervising patients in the community. There was no significant association between cessation of medication and involvement in incidents, rather the reverse. The decision to reduce or cease medication could, it seems, be taken more often but prudence suggests that this should be accompanied by frequent and continuous supervision.

It was suggested that rehabilitation programmes should be designed for various types of patients in consultation with those most concerned, and revised to suit the particular circumstances of individual patients preparing for discharge from either the Special or NHS hospital. Each should contain a series of goals and an approximate time during which all concerned think, in the light of this study and of subsequent consultation and experiment, that each goal might reasonably be achieved. It is essential that supervisors in the community should be consulted and involved in the planning of such programmes; and that nominated supervisors or agencies appointed should be involved and agree to the tailoring of programmes for any individual patient. No one would wish to be responsible for implementing a programme without having been previously involved. Most supervisors in the community very much wished for guidance and collaboration of some kind. Problems concerning medical ethics may have to be overcome when patients are transferred from the care of one doctor to another. The majority of psychiatrists interviewed had little experience with Special Hospital patients and would probably have appreciated some supportive collaborative exercise of the kind recommended. A few were eminent and experienced forensic psychiatrists whose engagement in this kind of interaction with the Special Hospital might facilitate the exchange of knowledge.

As soon as discharge has been recommended for restricted patients, that part of the programme which can be completed within the Special or NHS hospital could begin. If discharge is delayed for other than clinical reasons, day, weekend and other leave should be given from the Special Hospital or NHS hospital, in order to continue with the rehabilitation programme so far as is possible in the circumstances.

It may be objected that devising programmes for patients who may appear before a Mental Health Review Tribunal presents problems. There seems to be no reason why programmes devised to begin within a hospital should not be implemented when a Tribunal hearing is anticipated. Although it may then be manifest to all concerned that the patient would find difficulty in coping outside the hospital, some care and consultation may be necessary to avoid any suggestion that the programme is a test of such ability which would prejudice the decisions of the Review Tribunal. On the other hand, since some patients left the Special Hospital unexpectedly as a result of a Review Tribunal's decision (or as the result of a finding of not guilty after becoming fit to plead and a court hearing) it would seem advantageous to commence such a programme at an unstressful level with any patient remotely likely to leave.

Supervisions during the period of research were not preplanned to meet the individual needs of the variety of offenders who left the Special Hospital or the NHS hospitals after transfer. Many supervisors lacked the experience which would enable them to design a programme and the situation created anxieties in supervisors and resentment in patients. 'Off-the-peg' schemes for various groups of patients which can be adapted to suit individuals need to be created and evaluated for the benefit of patients and their families and helpers.

For example, although the Department of Health and Social Security claims that supervision has improved, there is no evidence that patients with a preadmission history of problem drinking are now receiving planned and evaluated attention and training which they probably need to forestall recurrance of their problem. Although some authorities consider that reformed problem drinkers can drink in moderation, the risks of disastrous consequences for a Special Hospital patient are high. It might be helpful if the Special and NHS hospitals endeavoured to foster in such patients attitudes towards alcohol which are inculcated in units specialising in addiction. This will only be practicable, it is certain, if the cooperation of all grades of staff and patients without drinking problems is obtained. If prohibition is seen as punitive, drink may be perceived as a reward. Social supervisors, it is suggested, need to be trained and medical supervisors supported in their supervision of these patients. A suitable programme might incorporate social skills training; collaboration between personnel inside and outside the Special Hospital (or the NHS hospital if a patient has first been transferred there) and with family or other unofficial helpers; day and other forms of leave; provision and use of accommodation other than hostels; planned employment or occupation; acquisition of practical skills; and the achievement of rapport with the prospective supervisor.

It was suggested that a predischarge programme of social skills training should be part of all rehabilitation programmes. It would be advisable to identify deficits and elicit patients' desired goals (Wilkinson, 1984, discusses methods). It should be practicable not only to teach the patient such skills but also to assist first choice helpers to acquire an understanding of the skills being taught and needing to be practised. Supervised day leave from the Special Hospital as well as NHS hospitals should be encouraged, under the care of supervisors or first choice helpers, so that patients can practise skills and engage in some of the activities which were described as alarming and stressful when encountered without preparation.

The kind of accommodation to which the patient is discharged may be important. Hostels are probably not the best placement and suggestions were mentioned above of ways in which hospitals might provide alternative accommodation. Self-contained flatlets might prove less stressful for patients than hostels and could, with some ingenuity, be managed at a distance from the hospital thus returning patients to their home areas and avoiding their reentry to the community amongst groups of stigmatised deviants.

Although employment may not facilitate reintegration, see page 101, some occupation was certainly thought by supervisors to prevent a return to drinking. Sometimes for example, unemployable patients who had been of considerable assistance to staff in long stay wards began drinking when they were discharged from hospital to a life which must then have seemed purposeless. It was interesting to note that some hospitals operated a policy which prevented them from employing discharged psychiatric patients, although the patients may have worked for them, usually at menial tasks for very little pay, whilst inpatients; others did successfully employ discharged patients, occasionally in positions of some responsibility. If NHS hospitals do not set an example in employing discharged patients it is not surprising that outside employers are sometimes reluctant to do so.

With the rise in unemployment the Special Hospital (and any NHS hospital which caters for longer staying patients) might turn its attention, like other establishments concerned with education and retraining, to the necessity of providing patients with the means to occupy themselves even if unemployed. Patients with talents in art and music found this no problem. Some skills such as plumbing, electrical repairs and car maintenance are still at a premium; window cleaners and gardeners were able to find employment in some areas and it might be sensible to shift to training for employment realistically available. Some opportunity to apply for work and for leave to take up employment would enable patients to qualify for insurance benefit and avoid embarrassment later. It would, however, be necessary to obtain skilled social work advice to avoid inpatient employment (often at low rates of pay) disqualifying patients for resettlement benefits at discharge. Patients also need to be prepared for the possibility that they will have to take uncongenial jobs and below standard accommodation. However, if housing can be provided in an area where work is more readily available this may be less of a problem. Other advantages of having several single units scattered geographically rather than grouping patients together have been mentioned above. Practical skills enabling men to shop, cook and clean for themselves, thus becoming independent despite long stays in hospital, should also be incorporated in any rehabilitation programme.

These recommendations and suggestions need to be discussed with those who would have to implement them and considered in the light of histories of those who relapse and those who do not. The aim should be to keep the patient busily occupied achieving a series of planned goals and his motivation to do so should be the discharge from formal supervision. The role of the supervisor(s) should be to help the patient to achieve these goals and to establish the rapport which will enable informal supervision to continue whilst the patient still feels the need for any support. In order to assist the patient to achieve goals, the chief helper must be able to establish rapport and shared aims with the patient; must adopt a positive attitude to patient progress in the community; and must be seen, in conjunction with other responsible agencies involved, to be working towards the patient's independence. Supervisions of patients in this study usually lasted for about three years, sometimes much less, occasionally far longer. Preparation for discharge, the establishment of supervisory rapport before discharge and an agreed rehabilitation programme should shorten this period. Social supervisors often changed after two years and it would be desirable to work towards an average goal of two years supervision in the community for this reason. Since relapses often occured after three years, however, those patients most at risk might expect to be supervised for rather longer. Some flexibility on the part of agencies might enable these more difficult and important supervisions whether formal or informal to continue whenever possible without interruption even if the supervisor has moved elsewhere. It would be desirable (and necessary if such supervisions are to be properly evaluated) for supervisors without experience, or with limited experience, to attend briefing courses before accepting responsibility for patients and to be willing to discuss progress of programmes at intervals so that these could be monitored. Such briefing courses could in due course be run by experienced supervisors in the various health areas and the suggested meetings of representatives to discuss progress would replace any central monitoring of experimental programmes.

A systematic development of such positive rehabilitatory schemes might reduce relapse by those most at risk who currently receive little support, give encouragement to those families who undertake the care of patients for whom little other provision is made, and facilitate liaison between supervisors at various stages in a patient's postdischarge career, thus avoiding the dangers of problems at transfer.

Conclusion

The problems of implementing recommendations for improving reintegration of Special Hospital patients can be foreseen. Research on this scale can only result in suggestions which those in the field will have the practical problem of putting into practice and evaluating. Interorganisational and interdisciplinary rivalries and antipathies which often resulted from misunderstandings might at least partly be resolved by a more systematic approach to programmed rehabilitation.

Previously, lack of information has led some supervisors to attribute failures in integration solely to traits in patients or to cessation of medication. One patient characteristic, problem drinking, was indeed associated with failure in reintegration. However, the findings emphasise the importance of other factors, especially the establishment of supervisory rapport and more frequent and continuous support at important stages in the patient's progress into the community. A more carefully planned approach to rehabilitation in the light of information concerning the importance of social factors might be more rewarding for supervisors, less expensive for the public purse and might very substantially reduce the incidence of failure for patients.

Appendix I
Measures used in the study

Measuring reintegration

Measures of integration used by some other research workers were thought inappropriate for patients in this study. Some, for example the Katz Adjustment scale (Thornberry and Jacoby, 1979), contained items likely to arouse anxiety. The use of recall, relapse and recidivism as measures without some other check has defects. Even if records were reliable, it was not at all certain that hospital admissions or offences with which patients are charged could be assumed to indicate levels of psychological adjustment for individuals. Thornberry and Jacoby (1979) noted 'serious deficiencies' in the use of police records; and Freeman and Simmons (1963) and Zitrin et al. (1976) concluded that social factors and not objective differences in social adjustment led to recall and conviction.

In this study it had been intended to rely very considerably upon the grid measure described below which is shown to reflect individual adjustment on important aspects. In the event there was a depressing lack of evidence of any association between positive aspects of reintegration shown by the grid and various kinds of supervision and training etc., mostly, it was concluded, because little specific effort was made to promote positive aspects by rehabilitation.

Because relatively few associations were found with the positive aspects of the grid measure, and because many more were found with the negative conventional indicators of recall, relapse and recidivism, negative indicators predominate in the analyses in this book. The grid measure has been most useful in examining patients' relationships with families and supervisors which could not otherwise have been explored and in facilitating the interpretation of other material, particularly concerning supervision. The grid measure did, however, coincide with clinical impressions for groups of patients whom doctors saw frequently; moreover, the division of the patients into two groups, better or less well integrated according to the grid measure, coincided with the negative incident measures generally reported throughout the book.

The grid measure has been explained in the text, see Chapters Two and Five, in sufficient detail to enable readers to assess the findings. In this appendix more details are given in the hope that practitioners and research workers might replicate the method. The evaluation of rehabilitation presents formidable difficulties and the use of a common measure might offer some possibility of comparisons. It is certainly hoped that future research may be conducted using this measure to evaluate the impact of more specific and positive forms of rehabilitation.

Measures of relapse and recidivism

For many patients only measures of relapse and recidivism were available, and these were certainly the only indicators which could be used for comparisons with some other studies. In the present study all formal or informal recalls or readmissions to hospital, and all attempted or completed suicides, were recorded as 'psychiatric incidents' which indicated relapse. All court appearances and prison admissions were recorded as 'criminal incidents' which indicated reoffending. (Other data on offending was also accumulated, including details of police contact, charges resulting from such contact, offences not resulting in court appearances, lengths of time till first offence, etc. and these were drawn upon for various aspects of the study not directly concerned with the establishment of a degree of integration).

Incidents, see Bowden's (1981) review, probably reflect life style, some patients appearing in court and some admitted to hospital for similar behaviour depending on the way in which the deviant activity is regarded by the patient, his family, friends or official helpers. Involvement in any such incidents proved to be associated with preadmission history, see the Tables in Appendix Two and pages 49-50 in the text. A system of weighting for gravity of incidents was devised as a more accurate indicator of the presence or absence of the kind of seriously deviant behaviour which treatment in the Special Hospital was intended to prevent. For example, recalls to Special Hospitals and suicide or attempted suicide attracted a weighting of 10; formal readmissions to hospital attracted a weighting of 2, and numerous or lengthy prison sentences, or convictions for serious offences (e.g. homicide, attempted homicide, sexual offences other than exhibitionism, arson, assaults) attracted weightings of between 3 and 5; and an informal hospital admission, or an appearance in court charged with a less serious offence other than a parking offence, attracted a weighting of one point.

Thus for every social factor eventually investigated it was possible to produce six tables showing the strengths of any association with patient involvement in (a) none, one, and two or more psychiatric incidents; (b) none, one, and two or more criminal incidents; (c) total numbers of patients involved in these numbers of psychiatric and criminal incidents; (d), (e) and (f) incidents as in (a), (b) and (c) weighted for gravity, see Table 2.1 and the Tables in Appendix Two. Categorisation was arranged so as to divide those involved in incidents into two roughly equal groups of those with few or multiple (or less serious and serious) involvements to simplify further analysis. This resulted in an attribution of 'seriousness' to events which could reasonably be regarded as 'serious' in common sense terms. The following, for example, were all 'serious': any offence other than an acquisitive or less serious offence; three informal readmissions to hospital, or two, if one was a formal admission; or recall or suicide. Possibly controversial differences amongst heavier weightings did not therefore affect analysis.

The form of repertory grid

Repertory grids are now familiar instruments in research as well as in psychological and psychiatric clinical practice, and a simple introduction to their use in research, including a bibliography of helpful texts for beginners, can be obtained from the Department of Sociology at the University of Surrey (Norris, 1982). The use of the grid measure and its validation by reference to the involvement of patients in incidents, and also to clinical and social workers' assessments of patient progress, were summarised in Chapter Two but details of the form and its administration were not included there.

The grid form used to study change

The grid form used was adapted from a grid employed as a 'before' and 'after' measure in previous studies investigating changes in self esteem and in attitudes towards rule breaking (deviant behaviour) and standing on one's own feet/depending on others (independence). Three studies dealt with such changes for the following subjects: mainly young, mostly male offenders and others in hostels endeavouring to implement therapeutic community approaches (Norris, 1979); young male offenders in a Detention Centre (Norris 1977a, 1977b); and older men and women patients in a hospital unit well known for its therapeutic community work with sociopaths and psychopaths (Norris, 1983a). In these earlier studies the grid was used as a repeated measure charting changes during a period of treatment or rehabilitation intended to reintegrate the recipients into the community. The grid was useful in the evaluation of various kinds of environmental treatment and also generated a typology of changes.

The grid measures attitude change but behaviour is not always predictable from attitudes. However, deviant behaviour and self percepts as rule breaking are closely associated according to authorities already cited in Chapter Two, page 12. The measure had coincided with independent judgements of social workers, therapists and clinicians in those earlier studies where such participants had made assessments (Norris, 1979 and 1983a). In the study where therapists were in closest contact with patients, interpretation of grid data coincided with unequivocal clinical impressions recorded at the end of treatment in 78 per cent of instances.

In previous studies the grid had been used as a 'before and after' measure reporting changes during treatment only. It was argued in the published reports that for theoretical reasons the incorporation in the measure of data concerning self esteem gave grounds for believing it to be predictive after treatment ended. It was thought that a follow up of the subjects in those studies could only be superficial and might be misleading if the effects of treatment were not considered in the light of a multiplicity of intervening variables which would probably affect behaviour. In this study the problem of intervening variables was to be dealt with by collecting all the information described in Chapter Three, but there were other difficulties.

It was not possible to obtain 'before and after' grid measures to examine changes in all patients from the time they left the Special Hospital until they were interviewed in the community because only a small proportion of patients left whilst the project was in progress, four-fifths having left earlier, that is before the project began in 1979. However, the grid does not have to be used as a repeated measure and by adapting the design it was possible to make a comparison over time using a single grid.

Composing and completing grids

Repertory grid technique is based on the work of Kelly (1955). His theoretical approach posits that individuals construct their own view of reality from the experience of testing personal hypotheses of how they themselves, or other people, will behave or how situations will develop, in familiar contexts.

Grids consist of a matrix recording relationships which the respondent reports. They usually incorporate a set of 'elements' (in this study, a selection of family, peers, doctor, social supervisor, plus three 'self' elements explained later in this section) along one side and a set of 'constructs' along the other. Elements were people of some significance in the patient's life and were supplied as 'roles' only, the names being elicited from the patient. Substitutes were accepted when, for instance, the patient had no family and could only name friends or acquaintances but analysis took such changes into account. Elements had been selected for earlier studies because of theoretical notions concerning the relationship between peers, family relationships, self percepts and deviant behaviour (see for example Downes, 1966; Davies, 1969; Glueck and Glueck, 1962; McCord and McCord, 1959; Mannheim, 1965; and Miller, 1958). For the current study other literature confirmed that similar relationships should be explored (see for example, Brown et al., 1972; Brown and Harris, 1978; Freeman and Simmons, 1963; Thornberry and Jacoby, 1979; Leff et al., 1982).

Two elements of particular interest were 'self' and 'ideal self'. In a series of studies (see Tannenbaum, 1938; Lemert, 1951; Hewitt, 1971; Reckless, 1957, 1960, 1961; Reckless and Dinitz, 1967; Schwartz and Tangri, 1965; Jensen, 1972; and Quinney, 1970) it has been argued that people with high self esteem, shown in the present study by the positive association of self with ideal self (with allowances made in some analyses of change for the fact that ideal self is not constant), are less likely to indulge in deviant behaviour and that a percept of self as not deviant acts as an insulator against deviant behaviour. Kaplan (1976) offers empirical evidence that high self esteem is predictive of socially acceptable behaviour. The acceptance of a self percept as deviant (breaks rules) is an important stage in the adoption of a deviant career, according to Lemert (1951), Becker (1963) and Wilkins (1964) amongst others. Self percept as independent (standing on own feet) may be related to self esteem and is of particular interest in this study because of the arguments by, for example, Goffman (1961), Clemmer (1962), Sykes (1958), Morris and Morris (1963), Cohen and Taylor (1972) and Sharp (1975) that custodial, institutional and therapeutic treatment can create dependency upon peers or custodians.

Constructs are bipolar ideas which a person has about the relationship between elements. These were mainly 'elicited' in the manner described below because of research evidence (see the review by Adams-Webber, 1970) that elicited elements and constructs produce more extreme relationships in grid patterns than those 'supplied' and are to be preferred when their use is feasible. It is also possible to determine the importance of 'supplied' elements and constructs for a patient when these are embedded in a grid of mainly 'elicited' material. Two constructs were supplied in the original form of the grid: 'breaks rules - doesn't break rules' and 'stands on own feet - depends on others'. A third, 'often criticises me - doesn't (hardly ever) criticise(s) me' was added to assist in investigating the role

151

of critical and probably emotionally involved helpers in this study.

Grids were completed in the same manner as in earlier studies. Element names were obtained by presenting the patient with a series of cards on which roles were written in capital letters. The patient was asked to provide names for these roles, where appropriate, from his own circle of 'significant others' and these were written on the cards. In the case of a few deaf patients instructions were written down. (Procedures can also be adapted for use with the illiterate and the mentally handicapped but this did not prove necessary during this study). Cards were used in order to make handling easy and to facilitate ranking in the next stage of the procedure.

Elicited constructs were obtained in a conventional manner, using triads of elements and asking the patient to say how two of the elements were alike in some way but differed from the third. The way in which they were alike was entered as the emergent pole (though sometimes reversed later in the analysis of some pairs of grids examined for change) and the implicit pole of the construct was either mentioned by the patient or could be discovered by questioning or during ranking when both poles of a construct would be clarified by the patient. In some cases where patients seemed to be having difficulties at the ranking stage, constructs could be eliminated or changed when they were seen to be inappropriate for technical reasons (for example, because they were 'impermeable' or not 'within the range of convenience' for some elements and therefore impossible to rank, see Fransella and Bannister, (1977) for explanations of these terms; or because two constructs were entwined and needed disentangling). Patients were asked to rank by arranging the element cards in rows. For instance if the patient offered 'bad tempered' and 'easy going' as one construct, he was asked to find the most bad tempered and the most easy going persons amongst the elements. These cards would be placed at the top and bottom of a row which the patient then completed by ranking in it all the other element cards. Once the first row has been completed most people can complete the procedure without assistance and the raw data can be recorded on grid forms (see Figures 1 and 2 at the end of this Appendix).

Adapting the grid for the Special Hospital study

In the present study, as has been explained, it was rarely possible to use the grid as a repeated measure. Instead, an element 'as I was when I left Broadmoor' (self at separation), was included in the grids to be completed in the community in addition to 'as I am now' (self) and 'as I would like to be' (ideal self). It was then possible for the patient to compare himself in the present time with himself at discharge, thus incorporating a comparison over time in a single grid. However, those patients who left Broadmoor during fieldwork completed a form of grid at the time of their departure (see Figure 2 at the end of this Appendix) which could be compared with the grid which they completed, like other patients in the community, some time after discharge (see Figure 1 at the end of this Appendix).

Analysing the grids

Two kinds of analysis were undertaken. One examined the single 'community grid' and this produced seven aspects of integration which were listed in Chapter Two, page 11. The second analysis was a purely technical exercise comparing 'separation grids' with 'community grids' where both were available from the same patient. The relationship between the retrospective element 'as I was when I left Broadmoor' in the community grid and the element 'as I am now' in the grid completed at the time of discharge was investigated. In addition there were now a number of 'before' and 'after' grids which, although their design differed slightly, could be compared to give measures of change over time like those in earlier studies. These findings were compared with the measure resulting from the single grid administered in the community.

The main focus was always upon the community grid which was intended in the first instance to produce a comparative measure of relative 'success' of patients in the community on seven aspects of integration, five of which were very similar to aspects of benefit used in the earlier studies; the additional two compared percepts of self at the date of interview with self at departure from Broadmoor.

Each aspect of integration was measured by examining the relationships of elements and constructs in the matrix. Slater's (1964, 1965, 1972) programmes were used for this analysis and a lucid explanation of the programme and analysis can be found in Pope and Keen (1981). In the earlier studies individual aspects of change on five factors (equivalent to aspects numbered 1,2,3,5 and 6 on page 11 of the text) were summed. Although this is methodologically suspect since it assumes that each factor is of equal weight the result led to an overall interpretation (of benefit where the number of aspects where treatment goals had been achieved outnumbered those where they had not; and of adverse effect where this situation was reversed) which had face value for social workers and therapists in the studies described above (Norris 1979 and 1983a). There seemed to be no reason, therefore, why the aspects of integration in this study, so closely related to the factors in the earlier studies, should not also be summed to give a score for each patient. The patients could then be divided into two groups, those better integrated with higher scores, and those less well integrated with lower scores. Individual scores were compared with supervisors' assessments, bearing in mind the tendency noted in earlier studies for social workers in particular to attribute benefit in a higher proportion of cases than the grid analysis showed. However, the measure was a relative one only, and was also compared with other indicators of success, including recidivism and readmission. The results of this analysis were reported in Chapter Two.

Analysis was then undertaken to discover if grids were recording changes since departure. Of the 145 grids collected, see page 9 of the text, 16 could be paired with a separation grid, fewer than had been anticipated. There were a smaller number of discharges during the period of fieldwork than had been estimated on the basis of previous figures and these patients, the most recent in the community, were less often available for interview since some were still in hospital and others reluctant to cooperate.

Separation grids were completed by patients with the assistance of members of the Psychology Department at the Special Hospital, community grids with the assistance of the interviewing team. Some minor problems were resolved (details can be consulted in the full report, Norris 1983b). These chiefly concerned procedures adopted for (a) effectively separating grid methodology from the collection of social factors and other data and (b) coping with one interviewer's difficulty in obtaining ranking.

A more substantial methodological problem arose when comparing some community grids with separation grids. Although both forms of grid included similar role elements, patients often wished to use new nominees for some roles when they completed the grid in the community. In order to preserve the integrity of those grids for comparison with other community grids, the most important part of the study, new nominations were accepted. This procedure did cast some doubt upon the comparability of community grids with grids completed at separation. On examination it was noted that the named social supervisor changed most frequently, and very often the doctor and friends were new nominees. Family members changed very rarely and it was hypothesised that if the role nominees were not constant they would not be central to variance in the construct system of the individual.

Results of preliminary analysis

Each grid was analysed by Slater's (1964) Ingrid programme and it was firstly ascertained that, as in earlier studies, the first three principal components accounted for most of the variance in all grids, so that attention to these three components only was justified. In this study 39 per cent of grids had 50 per cent or more variance accounted for by the first component, and another 40 per cent were within the 40 - 49 per cent range on the same component. 68 per cent had a further 20 - 35 per cent accounted for by the second component and 75 per cent had 10 - 20 per cent accounted for by the third component.

Supplied elements and constructs were then examined for

'importance' on these components. A construct or element was regarded as 'important' if it fell within the first quartile of weightings for this item on any of the patient's first three components, regardless of negative or positive affect. All the supplied constructs, and all elements of self with one exception, were 'important' on at least one of the first three components for between 70 per cent and 83 per cent of patients, varying according to the component. The element of self 'as I am now' appeared as not important on the first three components for 62 per cent of patients, a phenomenon to which reference will be made again later. It was not entirely unexpected since in an earlier study the importance of this self concept dropped between the 'before' and 'after' measure from 'not important' for 28 per cent of those concerned to 'not important' for 57 per cent (Norris, 1977a). Time did not permit investigation of this finding in 1977 but it appeared to have no consequence for the measure of change. It may be an indication of social anxiety; or it may indicate that patients in the present study were extremely selfconscious at the time of departure from the Special Hospital and subsequently perceived themselves as losing individuation, 'being lost in a crowd' after discharge (see Argyle, 1969, page 376).

It was concluded that analysis could proceed on the assumption that the principal features of the grid were of sufficient importance in the construct worlds of the patients concerned to justify drawing conclusions from relationships identified, but that some attention should be given to problems in analysis which might result from the low importance of self 'as I am now'.

For each community grid the relationships required to investigate the seven aspects of integration listed earlier were then examined:

If self 'as I am now' was closer to ideal self 'as I would like to be' than self at separation 'as I was when I left Broadmoor' then the patient scored 1 point for increased self esteem.

If self or ideal self was negatively related to 'breaks rules' the patient scored 1 point in each instance.

If self or ideal self was positively related to 'standing on own feet' (independence) the patient scored 1 point in each instance.

If self was more distantly related to 'breaks rules' than self at separation, the patient scored 1 point.

If self was more closely related to independence than self at separation, the patient scored 1 point.

Patients scoring seven points were more likely to be better integrated into the community than those scoring less. Variations in scores might demonstrate that patients could score low on aspects relating to independence but high on not breaking rules, suggesting an institutionalised adaptation; or the reverse might suggest a breaker of rules who would not make many demands upon the caring resources offered. This aspect of analysis is not, however, pursued in the text. It is not necessary to use Slater's programme to obtain these scores. Any convenient analysis may be adopted and practitioners with no other interest in grids could in most cases derive a crude score from an examination of the raw data.

Results of more detailed analysis of pairs of grids

Apart from the substantive findings it was of considerable interest to see whether the scores thus achieved resembled scoring which would have resulted from the use of the original measure of change had two grids been available for each patient and a rather complex analysis of the 16 pairs of grids was undertaken. In order to permit comparison, the community grid was reconstructed from the raw data by omitting from it the extra construct and two extra elements (as I was when I left Broadmoor' and 'person who helped me most since I left Broadmoor) which could not be included in the separation grid. A Delta programme was run for the pairs of ten by ten matrices thus available for each of 16 patients. The same techniques were used to generate five factor scores as in the previous studies and these were compared with the comparable aspects of the seven-fold score generated by use of the community grids only. Of 80 factors all but 14 coincided, 82 per cent congruity. Five of the incongruous factors were for one set of grids which appeared for inexplicable reasons to be totally dissimilar. On investigation it seemed that there had been some misunderstanding about the completion of the separation grid. If that pair of grids is excluded, all but nine of 75 comparable factors coincided, 88 per cent congruity.

Congruity resulted despite the fact, mentioned earlier, that persons named for element roles had changed. A similar analysis was undertaken which excluded any changed elements from both grids. There was very little difference in scores so derived, confirming the hypothesis that either 'role' was predominant over individuals named in the construct world of the individuals concerned or that where nominees changed they were not contributing much to the total variance in grids.

Considering the length of time which had elapsed between completion of separation and community grids, ranging from six months to nearly two years, the general degree of correlation between grids was surprisingly high. In previous studies a mean degree of correlation of .8 after a month and .7 after two months had been recorded. Over longer periods, of a year or more, a degree of correlation of between .5 and .6 was usual. In this study correlations between .5 and .7 were recorded for pairs of grids where four or less element names were changed, regardless of the time elapsed between grids.

Correlations of only .3 and .4 were found, as might be expected, in the four cases where five or six element names were changed, although the lower correlation did not affect congruity between the scores derived from such grids.

It was concluded that the measure derived from one grid taken in the community was very similar to that which would have been derived from repeated measures of the kind used in earlier studies. Moreover that the scores reflect changes in relationships between elements and constructs which are central to the patient's construct world.

The relationship between 'as I am now' in the separation grid (self at separation) and the same element in the community grid, 'as I was when I left Broadmoor', was examined. Again, community grids were reformed so that they could be compared with separation grids. The community grid was reformed as a ten by ten matrix as before but in this instance the 'self at separation' element was retained and the 'self as I am now' element removed. It should be noted that there is no methodological problem in reducing grids by excluding elements.

If the self at separation was accurately perceived at the later date in the community, there should have been little variance between that element and the self element in the separation grid. It was therefore disconcerting to find that although for some pairs this was the case, the mean variance over the sixteen pairs was very little less than might be expected by chance. Some very large variances were recorded. The explanation appeared to lie in the phenomenon already reported, that surprisingly little variance had been recorded between 'self as I am now' in the separation grid and in the community grid, a mean of less than 5 per cent, under half that which might occur by chance. Nevertheless, the scores obtained from the grids did show that changes in patients had occurred which were reflected both in changes between two grids and in the measure derived from the community grid. On reflection it seemed that this might have been forcseen. Self was recorded in preliminary analysis as 'not important' more often than other elements. It seemed that patients did not concern themselves as greatly with 'self' as with other elements in their construct world and perhaps they were reluctant to perceive changes in themselves. If patients changed since discharge or transfer in the ways scored for 'better integration', or the reverse, they might not in fact be very conscious of such changes. A patient might, after some lapse of time, revise his opinion of himself as he was when he left Broadmoor, an element which was important to most patients, in order to account for what he accurately perceived as changes in relationships in his construct world. Such a revision may accord with the perception of reality by others - that is, he may be thought to have had an incorrect view of his state at the time of discharge; but it will not affect either (a) the seven aspect measure taken from the static grid, which reflects differences perceived between self now and at separation; or (b) the measure of change derived from a repeated measure which ignores the retrospective view of self at separation altogether and only compares the shifts in the matrix for all relationships between self then and when in the community.

It may be that on aspects and factors involving relationship of self with other constructs and elements the distance in measures of change or the magnitude of the association in static measures may be underestimated. This is of no consequence for the analyses reported in this book which are only concerned with the direction of change or the positive or negative aspect of association. Comparisons of individual grid measures concerning magnitude present methodological problems which have been avoided by the directional analysis adopted by Norris for all studies using this grid form.

It is therefore argued that the seven aspect measure of change did accurately reflect changes since discharge, although patients revised their views of self at separation from Broadmoor rather than their current view of self, in order to account for changes.

Analysis of patient relationships

Importance of various people in the patient's construct world was derived from the relative salience of different elements. This can be established by examining the ranking of sums of squares of element deviation around construct means, and the first two of nine possible ranks were used to 'smooth' any chance oddities in distribution in the first rank. There were only minor differences when either one or two ranks were used.

Table 5.2 in the text shows the number of patients for whom various elements were ranked first in this manner. Table 5.3 shows the number of patients for whom various elements were in the first two ranks according to their closeness to 'ideal self' in the patient's construct world using interelement relationships expressed as cosines. These would be people with attributes which the patient regarded as those he would most like to have. Perceived similarity was found by ranking in a similar manner the first two elements closest to 'self' and the number of patients for whom various elements filled these ranks are shown in Table 5.4.

'Emotional involvement' for reasons explained in the text was found by locating the elements most closely related to the first pole of the construct 'often criticises me - doesn't (hardly ever) criticise(s) me' using cosines. Because the overwhelming predominance of 'disliked persons' in the first and second ranks squeezed out other roles which were of more importance to the analysis, elements in any of the first three ranks of closeness to the construct were used in the analysis of 'most critical' elements.

Table 5.9 shows the numbers of patients for whom various elements were 'most critical'. The aim was to identify elements perceived as most critical and no absolute standard was required; the use of three ranks did not greatly affect the order of elements.

Some other measures

For three aspects of postdischarge careers which were identified as of importance to respondents, scores were devised to facilitate comparison with indicators of reintegration.

Disclosure score

One was a 'disclosure score' which drew together all the information collected about the various people to whom patients might disclose their background (to first employers, last employers, hostel residents, parents, siblings, wife's parents, close friend, wife, children, social club members, group of friends or acquaintances, workmates) resulting in a figure giving actual disclosures as a percentage of possible disclosures. If the patient had no wife, friend, etc. that possibility was excluded from the total range of possible disclosures. Scores are shown below:

Appendix Table 1
Disclosure scores (as a percentage of possible disclosures)[*]
(N 327)

Scores	Number	Percent	Cumulative
0	36	11%	11%
17 - 29	8	2%	13%
30 - 59	42	13%	26%
60 - 79	55	17%	43%
80 - 99	35	11%	54%
100	151	46%	100%
Total	327	100%	100%

[*] Recoded as: 0 - 50 = 24%; 55 - 99 = 30%; 100 = 46% for analysis

'At risk' score

Another measure was an 'at risk' score roughly based on the findings of Leff et al. (1982) concerning frequent contact with emotionally involved relatives. 'At risk' points were awarded to patients who lived with a parent, wife or cohabitee or who saw such a relative very frequently; a point was added if either patient or relative was unemployed, two points if both were unemployed, because contact hours would be increased. Scores are shown overleaf.

159

Appendix Table 2
'At risk' scores (N 330)

Scores	Number	Per cent
0 No risk	234	71%
1 Very little risk (occasional meetings)	2	1%
2 Little risk (lives with, both employed)	24	7%
3 Some risk (lives with, one unemployed)	29	9%
4 High risk (lives with, both unemployed)	41	12%
Total	330	100%

Continuity of care score

Finally, a 'continuity of care' score was devised to test the
notion that interruption of supervision affected outcomes. It had
been noted during interviews that social supervisors regarded
supervision as uninterrupted if carried out by the same agency.
Patients on the other hand did not regard supervision as continuous
if supervisors had changed and there were some recorded cases where
relapse had occurred after a change which had been upsetting or
unsettling for the patient. One point was allotted for each year of
supervision, both medical and social, and one point was subtracted
for each change of supervisor, resulting in the folowing scores:

Appendix Table 3
Continuity of care score, active sample (N 330)

Score	Number	Percent	Cumulative
-9 to -6	6	2%	2%
-5 to -3	11	3%	5%
-2	13	4%	9%
-1	32	10%	19%
0	67	20%	39%
1	64	19%	58%
2	46	14%	72%
3	34	10%	82%
4	21	6%	88%
5 to 6	17	5%	93%
7 to 12	19	7%	100%

Collapsed to -9 to 0 (39%); 1 - 2 (33%); 3 to 12 (28%) for analysis.
Trials using other cut-off points did not affect reported analyses.

This concludes the Appendix describing measures used during the
study, apart from Figures A.1 and A.2 which follow and show the
design of the grid form used. Appendix Two contains a complete set
of six tables showing all types and scores for incidents.

CONSTRUCTS

1	2	3	4	5	6	7	8	9	10	11

ELEMENTS   Person nominated   Person nominated

1. As I am now   ....   11. As I was when I
2. Family member (f) ....   left S.H.   ....
3. Family member (m) ....   6. Person I dislike ....
4. Close (f) person   ....   7. Happy person   ....
5. Best (m) friend   ....   10. As I would like to be ....
12. Person who helped me most   8. Doctor   ....
    since I left S.H. ....   9. Social worker   ....

CONSTRUCTS

1. ....   6. ....
   ....
2. ....   7. ....
   ....
3.   Breaks rules   8.   Stands on own feet
     Doesn't break rules   Depends on others
4. ....   9. ....
   ....
5. ....   10. ....
   ....
            11. Often criticises me
                Hardly ever criticises me (or does not criticise me)

161

Figure A.2
Separation Grid

CONSTRUCTS

1	2	3	4	5	6	7	8	9	10

ELEMENTS Person nominated

1. As I am now ....
2. Family member (f) ....
3. Family member (m) ....
4. Close (f) person ....
5. Best (m) friend ....

Person nominated

6. Person I dislike ....
7. Happy person ....
10. As I would like to be ....
8. Doctor ....
9. Social worker ....

CONSTRUCTS

1. ....
....
2. ....
....
3. Breaks rules
Doesn't break rules
4. ....
....
5. ....
....
6. ....
....
7. ....
....
8. Stands on own feet
Depends on others
9. ....
....
10. ....
....

Appendix II
Incident scores by preadmission history

This appendix comprises a complete set of six tables showing one variable, preadmission history, by all six types of incident score. Full tabulations of this kind for every factor would have been cumbersome in the text but some tables extracted from similar sets for other variables are occasionally included there, for example, Tables 4.3 and 4.4. More often only the summary of significance and strengths of association which appear at the foot of each table are listed and the direction of association is discussed in the text, with illustrative percentages when necessary.

Appendix Table 4
Preadmission history by frequency of postdischarge psychiatric incidents

	Postdischarge incidents		
Preadmission history	None	One	Two +
Court appearances and			
hospital admissions	69 (55%)	33 (26%)	24 (19%)
Court appearances only	64 (67%)	21 (22%)	11 (12%)
Hospital admissions only	42 (60%)	18 (26%)	10 (14%)
None known	32 (84%)	4 (11%)	2 (5%)
Total (N330)	207 (63%)	76 (23%)	47 (14%)

$$\chi^2 = 12.51, \text{ df } 6, \text{ p} < .05; \text{ Cramer's V } .13$$

Appendix Table 5
Preadmission history by seriousness of (weighted) postdischarge
psychiatric incidents

	Weighted incidents		
Preadmission history	Nil	1–2	3–22
Court appearances and hospital admissions	69 (55%)	22 (18%)	35 (28%)
Court appearances only	64 (67%)	10 (10%)	22 (23%)
Hospital admissions only	42 (60%)	15 (21%)	13 (19%)
None known	32 (84%)	3 (8%)	3 (8%)
Total (N330)	207 (63%)	50 (15%)	73 (22%)

x^2=15.12, df 6, p<.01; Cramer's V .15

Appendix Table 6
Preadmission history by frequency of postdischarge criminal incidents

	Postdischarge incidents		
Preadmission history	None	One	Two +
Court appearances and hospital admissions	87 (69%)	20 (16%)	19 (16%)
Court appearances only	62 (65%)	19 (20%)	15 (16%)
Hospital admissions only	59 (84%)	8 (11%)	3 (4%)
None known	32 (84%)	6 (16%)	0 (0%)
Total (N330)	240 (73%)	53 (16%)	37 (11%)

x^2=15.46, df 6, p<.02; Cramer's V .15

Appendix Table 7
Preadmission history by seriousness of (weighted) postdischarge
criminal incidents

	Weighted incidents		
Preadmission history	Nil	1–2	3–11
Court appearances and hospital admissions	87 (69%)	19 (15%)	20 (16%)
Court appearances only	62 (65%)	10 (10%)	24 (25%)
Hospital admissions only	59 (84%)	7 (10%)	4 (6%)
None known	32 (84%)	2 (5%)	4 (11%)
Total (N330)	240 (73%)	38 (12%)	52 (16%)

x^2=18.03, df 6, p<.006; Cramer's V .17

Appendix Table 8
Preadmission history by frequency of all postdischarge incidents

Preadmission history	Postdischarge incidents		
	None	One	Two +
Court appearances and hospital admissions	53 (42%)	27 (21%)	46 (37%)
Court appearances only	40 (42%)	25 (26%)	31 (32%)
Hospital admissions only	39 (56%)	13 (19%)	18 (26%)
None known	29 (76%)	4 (11%)	5 (13%)
Total (N330)	161 (49%)	69 (21%)	100 (30%)

X^2=18.02, df 6, p<.006; Cramer's V .17

Appendix Table 9
Preadmission history by seriousness of all (weighted) postdischarge incidents

Preadmission history	Weighted incidents		
	Nil	1-3	4-22*
Court appearances and hospital admissions	53 (42%)	32 (21%)	41 (37%)
Court appearances only	40 (42%)	16 (17%)	40 (42%)
Hospital admissions only	39 (56%)	20 (29%)	11 (16%)
None known	29 (76%)	3 (8%)	6 (16%)
Total (N330)	161 (49%)	71 (21%)	98 (30%)

X^2=27.64, df 6, p<.001; Cramer's V .20

* See page 50 for an explanation of the rationale for this weighting.

Bibliography

Adams-Webber, J.R., (1970), 'Elicited versus provided constructs in repertory grid technique: a review', British Journal of Medical Psychology, vol.43, pp.349-354.

Argyle, M., (1969), Social Interaction, Methuen, London.

Acres, D., (1975), The After-Care of Special Hospital Patients, Appendix 3 in HMSO (1975), The Butler Report, pp.291-302.

Association of Directors of Social Services, (1981), 'Turnover of social work staff, length of time social workers have been in post, the ages of social workers and limits on social workers' responsibilities', survey for the Barclay Committee, Newcastle.

Becker, H.S., (1963), Outsiders: Studies in the Sociology of Deviance, Free Press, New York.

Bergin, A. and Strupp, H., (1972), Changing Frontiers in the Science of Psychotherapy, Aldine Atherton, Chicago.

Berscheid, E. and Walster, E.H., (1969), Interpersonal Attraction, Addison-Wesley, Reading, Mass.

Black, D.A., (1982), 'A five year follow-up study of male patients discharged from Broadmoor Hospital 1960-65' in Gunn, J., and Farrington, D.P., (eds.), Abnormal Offenders, Delinquency and the Criminal Justice System, Wiley, New York.

Bowden, P., (1981), 'The Fate of Special Hospital Patients', British Journal of Psychiatry, vol.138, pp.340-354.

Brown, G.W., Birley, J.L.T. and Wing, J.K., (1972), 'Influence of Family Life on the Course of Schizophrenic Disorders: a Replication', British Journal of Psychiatry, vol.121, pp.241-258.

166

Brown, G.W. and Harris, T., (1978), Social Origins of Depression, Tavistock, London.

Brown, G.W., Monck, E.M., Carstairs, G.M. and Wing, J.K., (1962), 'Influence of Family Life on the Course of Schizophrenic Illness', British Journal of Preventive Social Medicine, vol.16, pp.55-68.

Byrne, D., (1962), 'Response to attitude similarity-dissimilarity as a function of affiliation need', Journal of Personality, vol.30, pp.164-177.

Byrne, D., (1971), The Attraction Paradigm, Academic Press, London.

Byrne, D. and Nelson D., (1965), 'Attraction as a linear function of proportion of positive reinforcements', Journal of Personal and Social Psychology, vol.1, pp.659-663.

Cicourel, A., (1968), The Organisation of Juvenile Justice, Wiley, New York.

Clemmer, D., (1962), 'Prisonization' in Wolfgang, M.E., Savitz, L.D. and Johnston O., (eds.), The Sociology of Punishment and Correction, Free Press, New York.

Cohen, S. and Taylor, L., (1972), Psychological Survival, Penguin, London.

Collis, M. and Ekdawi, M.Y., (1983), The Relatives' Story, Netherne Hospital Monograph, Coulsdon, Surrey.

Collis, M. and Ekdawi, M.Y., (1982), Psychiatric Rehabilitation: Needs of a Health District, (unpublished ms.), Netherne Hospital, Coulsdon, Surrey.

Cooper, D., (1971), The Death of the Family, Penguin, London.

Davies, M., (1969), Probationers in their Social Environment, Home Office Research Unit Report, no.21, HMSO, London.

Dell, S., (1980), The Transfer of Special Hospital Patients to NHS Hospitals, Special Hospital Research Report, no. 16, London.

DHSS, (1978), Collaboration in Community Care - A Discussion Document, HMSO, London.

Dittes, J.E., (1959), 'Attractiveness of group as function of self-esteem and acceptance by group', Journal of Abnormal and Social Psychology, vol.59, pp.77-82.

Downes, D., (1966), The Delinquent Solution, Routledge and Kegan Paul, London.

Duck, S.W. and Craig, G., (1978), 'Personality Similarity and the Development of Friendship', British Journal of Social and Clinical Psychology, vol.17, pp.237-242.

Fransella, F. and Bannister, D., (1977), A Manual for Repertory Grid Technique, Academic Press, London.

Freeman, H.E. and Simmons, O.G., (1963), The Mental Patient Comes Home, Wiley, New York.

Garfinkel, H., (1967), 'Good Organisational Reasons for Bad Clinic Records', Studies in Ethnomethodology, Prentice Hall, New York.

Glueck, S. and Glueck, E., (1962), Family Environment and Delinquency, Routledge and Kegan Paul, London and New York.

Goffman, E., (1961), Asylums, Penguin, London.

Gostin, L.O., (1977), A Human Condition, MIND, London.

167

Henderson, A.S., (1974), 'Care-eliciting Behaviour in Man', _Journal of Nervous and Mental Diseases_, vol.159, pp.172-181.

Henderson, A.S., (1977), 'The Social Network, Support and Neurosis', _British Journal of Psychiatry_, vol.131, pp.185-191.

Henderson, A.S., (1978), 'The Patient's Primary Group',_British Journal of Psychiatry_, vol.132, pp.74-86.

HMSO (1973), _Report on the Review of Procedures for the Discharge and Supervision of Psychiatric Patients Subject to Special Restrictions_, Cmnd.5191, ('The Aarvold Report'), London.

HMSO (1975), _Report of the Committee on Mentally Abnormal Offenders_, Cmnd.6244, ('The Butler Report'), London.

Hewitt, J.P., (1971), _Social Stratification and Deviant Behaviour_, Random House, New York.

Huntingdon, J., (1981), _Social Work and General Medical Practice: Collaboration or Conflict?_, Allen and Unwin, London.

Jensen, G.F., (1972), 'Delinquency amd adolescent self-conceptions: a study of the personal relevance of infraction', _Social Problems_, vol.20, pp.84-102.

Kaplan, H.B., (1976), 'Self-attitudes and deviant response', _Social Forces_, vol.54, pp.788-901.

Kelly, G.A., (1955), _The Psychology of Personal Constructs, Vols.I and II_, Norton, New York.

Kelman, H.C., (1966), 'Three Processes of Social Influence' in Jahoda, M. and Warren, N. (eds), _Attitudes_, Penguin, London.

Laing, R.D. and Esterson, A., (1964), _Sanity, Madness and the Family_, Tavistock, London.

Leff, J.P., (1976), 'Schizophrenia and Sensitivity to the Family Environment', _Schizophrenia Bulletin_, vol.2, pp.566-574.

Leff, J.P., Kuipers, L., Berkowitz, R., Eberlen-Vries, R. and Sturgeon, D., (1982), 'Controlled Trial of Social Intervention in the Families of Schizophrenic Patients', _British Journal of Psychiatry_, vol.141, pp.121-134.

Leff, J.P. and Vaughn, C., (1981), 'The role of maintenance therapy and relatives' expressed emotion in relapse in schizophrenia: a two-year follow-up', _British Journal of Psychiatry_, vol.139, pp.102-104.

Lemert, E.M., (1951), _Social Pathology_, McGraw Hill, New York.

Mackie, A.J., (1981), 'Attachment Theory: Its relevance to the therapeutic alliance', _British Journal of Medical Psychology_, vol.54, pp.203-212.

McCord, W. and McCord, J., (1956), _Psychopathy and Delinquency_, Grune and Stratton, New York.

Mannheim, H., (1965), _Comparative Criminology_, Routledge and Kegan Paul, London and New York.

Miller, W.B., (1958), 'Lower class culture as a generating milieu of gang delinquency', _Journal of Social Issues_, vol.14.

Morris, T.P. and Morris, P., (1963), _Pentonville_, Routledge and Kegan Paul, London.

Newcomb, T.M., (1961), _The Acquaintance Process_, Holt, Rinehart and Winston, New York.

Norris, M., (1977a), 'Construing in a Detention Centre', in New Perspectives in Personal Construct Theory, Bannister, D, (ed.), Academic Press, London.

Norris, M., (1977b), 'Use of repertory grid in investigating change in trainees at a Detention Centre', British Journal of Criminology, vol.17, pp. 274-279.

Norris, M., (1978), 'Those we like to help', New Society, vol.45, p.18.

Norris, M., (1979), 'Offenders in Residential Communities - Measuring and Understanding Change', Howard Journal, vol. xviii, pp.29-43.

Norris, M., (1981), 'Problems in the Analysis of Soft Data and Some Suggested Solutions', Sociology, vol.15, pp.337-51.

Norris, M., (1982), Beginner's Guide to the Use of Repertory Grids in Research, Occasional Paper No.1, Department of Sociology, University of Surrey, Guildford.

Norris, M., (1983a), 'Changes in patients during treatment at the Henderson Hospital therapeutic community during 1977-81', British Journal of Medical Psychology, vol.56, pp.135-143.

Norris, M., (1983b), 'Final Report on Social Factors Associated with the Re-integration into the Community of Ex-Special Hospital Patients - Parts One to Eight', as presented to the Department of Health and Social Security 1982-1983, unpublished, available University of Surrey Library, Guildford.

Novak, D.W. and Lerner, M.J., (1968), 'Rejection as a consequence of perceived similarity', Journal of Personality and Social Psychology, vol.9, pp.147-52.

Otto, S. and Orford, J., (1978), Not Quite Like Home: Small Hostels for Alcoholics and Others, Wiley, Chichester.

Pope, M. and Keen, T., (1981), Personal Construct Psychology and Education, Academic Press, London.

Quinney, R., (1977), The Social Reality of Crime, Little Brown, Boston, Mass.

Reckless, W.C., (1957), 'The self component in potential delinquency and potential non-delinquency', American Sociological Review, vol.22, pp.566-70.

Reckless, W.C., (1960), 'The good boy in a high delinquency area', Journal of Criminal Law, Criminology and Police Science, vol.48, pp18-26.

Reckless, W.C., (1961), 'A new theory of delinquency and crime', Federal Probation, vol.25, pp.42-6.

Reckless, W.C. and Dinitz, S., (1967), 'Pioneering with self concept as a vulnerability factor in delinquency' Journal of Criminal Law, Criminology and Police Science, vol.59, pp.515-23.

Rogers, C.R., (1951), Client-centred Therapy, Houghton Mifflin, New York.

Schwarz, M. and Tangri, S.S., (1965), 'A note on self concept as an insulator against delinquency', American Sociological Review, vol.20, pp.922-6.

Scott, J., (1979), 'Reflections upon the characteristics of social work with families of Special Hospital patients', unpublished MA dissertation, Brunel University, Uxbridge.

Sharp, V., (1975), Social Control in the Therapeutic Community, Saxon House, London.

Slater, P., (1964), The Principal Components of a Repertory Grid, Vincent Andrews, London.

Slater, P., (1965), 'The use of Repertory Grid Technique in the Individual Case', British Journal of Psychiatry, vol. III, pp.965-975.

Slater, P., (1972), Composite diagrams and systems of angular relationships applying to grids, (mimeographed), St George's Hospital, London.

Sykes, G., (1958), The Society of Captives, Princeton University Press, Princeton, N.J.

Tannenbaum, F., (1938), Crime and Community, Columbia University Press, New York.

Thornberry, T.P. and Jacoby, J.E., (1979), The Criminally Insane, University of Chicago Press, Chicago, Ill.

Truax C.B. and Carkhuff R.R., (1967), Towards Effective Counselling and Psychotherapy, Aldine, New York.

Vaughan, P.J., (1980), 'Letters and visits to long-stay Broadmoor patients', British Journal of Social Work, vol.10, pp.471-481.

Vaughn, C. and Leff, J.P., (1976a), 'The Influence of Family and Social Factors on the Course of Psychiatric Illness: a Comparison of Schizophrenic and Depressive Neurotic Patients', British Journal of Psychiatry, vol.129, pp.129-137.

Vaughn, C. and Leff, J.P., (1976b) 'The measurement of EE in Families of Psychiatric Patients', British Journal of Social and Clinical Psychology, vol.15, pp.157-165.

Walker, N. and McCabe, S., (1973), Crime and Insanity in England, VII: New Solutions - New Problems, Edinburgh University Press.

Walster, E., (1965), 'The effect of self-esteem on romantic liking', Journal of Experimental Social Psychology, vol.1, pp.184-97.

Wilkins, L.T., (1964), Social Policy, Action and Research, Tavistock, London.

Wilkinson, J.D., (1984), The Assessment of Social Skill in a Schizophrenic Out-patient Population, (PhD thesis in preparation) University of Surrey, Guildford.

Zitrin, A. et al., (1976), 'Crime and Violence Among Mental Patients', American Journal of Psychiatry, vol.133, pp.142-9.

Author index

Subject index

Active sample 11,15-16,23,29-34,43-45,49-85,86-115,116-125,130,160
Activity 76,77-78
  criminal 25,34,68,69,74,109,129
Absolute discharge (AD) 5,6,15,24,35,36,64,106,116-121
Accommodation 27-30,34,43,46,48,57,**58**,70,87,**101-104**,112,115,124,126,
  134,140,144,145
Acquisitive offence 20,22,23,25,45,54,61,62,77,80,102,117,149
Admission diagnosis 21-25,**51**,52-60,77-78,83,100,130-131,132,138
  and see diagnosis
Admission offence 20-23,47,55,**61-62**,68,69,72,73,76-77,85,102,112,
  117,120,126,129,131
Aftercare 2,65,111,124,126,128,135
Age 19,26,27,47,**60-61**,65,66,67,69,72,74,**78**,80,81,88,95,103,104,109
  114,119,121,122,125,126,129
Agency(cies), social work 9,19,39,41-43,52,110,112,140,142,145,160
Alcohol abuse, see ' drinking problem'
Alone, living 29,**30**,102,124
Arson 20,22,23,25,54-55,62,77,80,102,117,129,149
Assault 11,20,22,23,25,54-55,62,69,73,77,80,102,112,117,119,120,129
  131,149
At risk 42,86-87,98-99,**114**,115,121-122,129,138,145,159-160
Attitude 5,74,77,**78**,86,87,94-95,96,130,136,139,140,143,145,150

Broadmoor 1-2,**4**,5-6,8,11,15-17,18,21,29,30,33,34,36,44,61,65,71,74,
  76,104,119,122,123,124,126,138,139

Career, see 'postdischarge career'
Characteristic
  changed since 1960's 2,4,41,116-121
  patient 1-4,**18,19,20**,37,46,47,65,71,74,78,81,82,85,86,120,121,126,
    127,129,146
Close relative 89-99,102,104,114-115,120,132-133
  and see 'family', 'parent'
Comparative study 1-4,**116-126**
Condition of Restriction Order 6,35,37-38,41,73,93,106,124,134
Conditional discharge (CD, formal discharge) 5-6,15,24,35,116-121
  and see 'formal supervision'
Contact with close relative 88-89,98,115,133-134
Contact with psychiatrist, doctor 12,28,37-38,40,53,63,104,108-110,
    115,150
Contact with social supervisor 12,104,107-108,115
  and see 'frequency', 'at risk'
Continuity of care 40,46,65,107,**109**,110-111,141,160
  medical 12,**109-111**
  social 12,**109-111**
Core sample 15-16,23,24,44,75,77
Court appearance 45,49,50,52,63,79,81,119,123,125,126,143,149,
    163-165
  and see 'incident, criminal' and 'preadmission history'
Criminal postdischarge incident, see 'incident, criminal'
Criminal preadmission history, see 'preadmission history'
Critical doctor 97-98,115
Critical element 97,158
Critical helper 97-98,115,133,152
Critical relative 97-98,133
Critical social supervisor 97-98,115
Criticism **96,98**
  and see 'expressed emotion'

Dangerous 2,11,37,45,63
Data, collection 4,**8-10**,45
  hard 8,10,48
  soft 8,9,48,104,140
Death 5,15,16,19,45
  and see 'suicide'
Department of Health and Social Security (DHSS) 38,39,86,134,135,
    136,137,138,143
Dependence 11,30,78,83,124,151
  and see 'independence'
Deported 5,15
Deviant behaviour 3,25,37,46,**52**,54,61,66,70,103,105-109,111,115,118,
    121,125-126,129,135,148-151
Diagnosis 13,19-20,21,23,44,46,47,48,**51-60**,61,72,73,74,75,76,77,78,
    81,83,85,89,**98**,99,101,102-104,110,114,117,121,123,**130**,131,132,138
  and see 'admission diagnosis'
Disability 18,21,31,46,125

Postdischarge offence, criminal history, **43,44**
  and see 'incident, criminal, frequent, serious'
Postdischarge relapse, psychiatric history, **43,45**
  and see 'incident, psychiatric, frequent, serious'
Preadmission history 3–4,**18**,20,21,25,26,45,47,**49–51**,60,62,72,73–74,
    85,121,122–124,129,148,163–165
  and see 'criminal preadmission history', 'history', psychiatric
  preadmission history'
Prison 5,10,15,19,20,21,28,46,56,63,105,107,119,125,135,139,149
  and see 'HMP'
Probation officer, service 3,28,35,39–40,41,42,52,91,95,136
  and see 'social supervisor'
Problem 19,20,26,30,32–33,53,64–65,70,82,87,101,111–112,113,127,129,
    133,141,142,145,146
  at transfer, or other change of status 64,**111–112**,146
  and see 'financial', 'drinking problem'
Psychiatric hospital, see 'NHS hospital'
Psychiatric illness, see 'mental illness'
Psychiatric incident, see 'incident, psychiatric'
Psychiatric patient 2,29,45,88,**116**,134,144
Psychiatric preadmission history, see 'preadmission history'
Psychiatric supervision, see 'medical supervision'
Psychiatrist 2,6,35,36,38,44,53,54,64,70,108,124,136,139,143
  and see 'doctor'
Psychologist 86,124,141
Psychopath(ic) 13,19,21,24,25,26,36,44,51–60,65–69,73,75,77,78,80,
    81,83,84–85,89,98–99,102–104,106,109,110,111,114,115,117,118,119,
    120–121,129,130,131,133
Psychopathy (personality disorder) 1,24,74,99,103,118,121,130,131
  and see 'diagnosis'

Rapport 79,**87**,89,95,95,99,110,111,115,136,141,145,146
Readmission to hospital, see 'hospital readmission'
Recall 4,6,10,15,26,38,44,63,74,79,83,93,105,119,120,129,147,148,149
Recidivism 2,10,11,12,17,45,46,47,61,63,64,69,74,81,101,107,115,**119**,
    121,123,126,130,135,136,147,**148–149**
Recommendation 38,**137**,138–146
Rehabilitation 2,7,17,24,27,30,32–33,40,**55–56**,86,89,109,110,132,134,
    137,139–143,145,146,150
Reintegration 2,3,**10**,11–14,17,31,79,**82**,85,87,94–95,98,101,110–111,
    114,115,144,146,**147**,159
  and see 'integration'
Relapse 10,11,12,17,28,30,42,45,46,47,51,61,63,65,68,69,72,**81**,82,84,
    88,89,99,101,102,104,106,112,114–115,**119**,121,128,129,130,135,136,
    138,145,147,**148–149**,160
  and see 'incident, psychiatric'
Relationship, collaborative 38–40,136
  social 30,57,**58**,**87**,104,141,148,151,**158**
  with helper 9,35,38,**87–99**,110,141,**158**